Inside Steve's Brain

Leander Kahney is news editor for Wired.com and primary author of its popular *Cult of Mac* blog. He is also the author of two acclaimed books, *The Cult of Mac* and *The Cult of iPod*. As a reporter and editor, Kahney has covered Apple for more than a dozen years.

Inside
Steve's
Brain

Leander Kahney

Atlantic Books
London

First published in the United States of America in 2008 by Portfolio, a member of Penguin Group (USA) Inc.

First published in paperback in Great Britain in 2009 by Atlantic Books, an imprint of Grove Atlantic Ltd.

This paperback edition published in Great Britain in 2011 by Atlantic Books, an imprint of Atlantic Books Ltd.

1 2 3 4 5 6 7 8 9

A CIP catalogue record for this book is available from the British Library.

ISBN: 978 0 85789 717 6

Set in Vendetta with Myriad Pro
Designed by Daniel Lagin

Printed in Great Britain by Clays Ltd, St Ives plc

Atlantic Books
An imprint of Atlantic Books Ltd
Ormond House
26–27 Boswell Street
London
WC1N 3JZ

www.atlantic-books.co.uk

For my children, Nadine, Milo, Olin, and Lyle; my wife, Traci; my mother, Pauline; and my brothers, Alex and Chris. And Hank, my dear old dad, who was a big Steve Jobs fan.

Contents

Inside Steve's Brain

Introduction

"Apple has some tremendous assets, but I believe without some attention, the company could, could, could—I'm searching for the right word—could, could die."

—Steve Jobs on his return to Apple as interim CEO, in *Time*, August 18, 1997

Steve Jobs gives almost as much thought to the cardboard boxes his gadgets come in as the products themselves. This is not for reasons of taste or elegance—though that's part of it. To Jobs, the act of pulling a product from its box is an important part of the user experience, and like everything else he does, it's very carefully thought out.

Jobs sees product packaging as a helpful way to introduce new, unfamiliar technology to consumers. Take the original Mac, which shipped in 1984. Nobody at the time had seen anything like it. It was controlled by this weird pointing thing—a mouse—not a keyboard like other early PCs. To familiarize new users with the mouse, Jobs made sure it was packaged separately in its own compartment. Forcing the user to unpack the mouse—to pick it up and plug it in—would make it a little less alien when they had to use it for the first time. In the years since, Jobs has carefully designed this "unpacking routine" for each and every Apple product. The iMac packaging was designed to make it obvious how to get the machine on the Internet, and included a polystyrene insert specially designed to double as a prop for the slim instruction manual.

As well as the packaging, Jobs controls every other aspect of the customer experience—from the TV ads that stimulate desire for Apple's products, to the museum-like retail stores where customers buy them; from the easy-to-use software that runs the iPhone, to the online iTunes music store that fills it with songs and videos.

Jobs is a control freak extraordinaire. He's also a perfectionist, an elitist, and a taskmaster to employees. By most accounts, Jobs is a borderline loony. He is portrayed as a basket case who fires people in elevators, manipulates partners, and takes credit for others' achievements.[1] Recent biographies paint an unflattering portrait of a sociopath motivated by the basest desires—to control, to abuse, to dominate. Most books about Jobs are depressing reads. They're dismissive, little more than catalogs of tantrums and abuse. No wonder he's called them "hatchet jobs." Where's the genius?

Clearly he's doing something right. Jobs pulled Apple from

the brink of bankruptcy, and in ten years he's made the company bigger and healthier than it's ever been. He's tripled Apple's annual sales, doubled the Mac's market share, and increased Apple's stock 1,300 percent. Apple is making more money and shipping more computers than ever before, thanks to a string of hit products—and one giant blockbuster.

Introduced in October 2001, the iPod transformed Apple. And just as Apple has been transformed from a struggling also-ran into a global powerhouse, so has the iPod been transformed from an expensive geek luxury into a diverse and important product category. Jobs quickly turned the iPod from an expensive, Mac-only music player that many people dismissed into a global, multibillion-dollar industry that supports hundreds of accessory companies and supporting players.

Quickly and ruthlessly, Jobs updated the iPod with ever newer and better models, adding an online store, Windows compatibility, and then video. The result: more than 100 million sold by April 2007, which accounts for just under half of Apple's ballooning revenues. The iPhone, an iPod that makes phone calls and surfs the Net, looks set to become another monster hit. Launched in June 2006, the iPhone is already radically transforming the massive cell phone business, which pundits are saying has already divided into two eras: pre-iPhone and post-iPhone.

Consider a few numbers. At the time of this writing (November 2007) Apple had sold a whopping 100 million iPods, and is on track to ship more than 200 million iPods by the end of 2008 and 300 million by the close of 2009. Some analysts think the iPod could sell 500 million units before the market is saturated. All of which would make the iPod a contender for the biggest consumer electronics hit of all time. The current record holder, Sony's Walkman, sold 350 million units during its fifteen-year reign in the 1980s and early 1990s.

Apple has a Microsoft-like monopoly on the MP3 player market. In the United States, the iPod has nearly 90 percent market share: nine out of ten of all music players sold is an iPod.[2] Three quarters of all 2007 model year cars have iPod connectivity. Not MP3 connectivity, iPod connectivity. Apple has distributed 600 million copies of its iTunes jukebox software, and the iTunes online store has sold three billion songs. "We're pretty amazed at this," said Jobs at a press event in August 2007, where he cited these numbers. The iTunes music store sells five million songs a day—80 percent of all digital music sold online. It's the third largest music retailer in the United States, just behind Wal-Mart and Best Buy. By the time you read this, these numbers will probably have doubled. The iPod has become an unstoppable juggernaut that not even Microsoft can compete with.

And then there's Pixar. In 1995, Jobs's private little movie studio made the first fully computer-animated movie, *Toy Story*. It was the first in a string of blockbusters that were released once a year, every year, regular and dependable as clockwork. Disney bought Pixar in 2006 for a whopping $7.4 billion. Most important, it made Jobs Disney's largest individual shareholder and the most important nerd in Hollywood. "He is the Henry J. Kaiser or Walt Disney of this era,"[3] said Kevin Starr, a culture historian and the California state librarian.

What a remarkable career Jobs has had. He's making an immense impact on computers, on culture, and, naturally, on Apple. Oh, and he's a self-made billionaire, one of the richest men in the world. "Within this class of computers we call personals he may have been, and continues to be, the most influential innovator," says Gordon Bell, the legendary computer scientist and a preeminent computer historian.[4]

But Jobs should have disappeared years ago—in 1985, to be precise—when he was forced out of Apple after a failed power struggle to run the company.

Born in San Francisco in February 1955 to a pair of unmarried graduate students, Steve was put up for adoption within a week of his birth. He was adopted by Paul and Clara Jobs, a blue-collar couple who soon after moved to Mountain View, California, a rural town full of fruit orchards that didn't stay rural very long—Silicon Valley grew up around it.

At school, Steven Paul Jobs, named after his adoptive father, a machinist, was a borderline delinquent. He says his fourth-grade teacher saved him as a student by bribing him with money and candy. "I would absolutely have ended up in jail," he said. A neighbor down the street introduced him to the wonders of electronics, giving him Heathkits (hobbyist electronics kits), which taught him about the inner workings of products. Even complex things like TVs were no longer enigmatic. "These things were not mysteries anymore," he said. "[It] became much more clear that they were the results of human creation, not these magical things."[5]

Jobs's birth parents had made attending college a condition of his adoption, but he dropped out of Reed College in Oregon after the first semester, although he continued to unofficially attend classes in subjects that interested him, like calligraphy. Penniless, he recycled Coke bottles, slept on friends' floors, and ate for free at the local Hare Krishna temple. He experimented with an all-apple diet, which he thought might allow him to stop bathing. It didn't.

Jobs returned to California and briefly took a job at Atari, one of the first games companies, to save money for a trip to India. He soon quit and headed out with a childhood friend in search of enlightenment.

On his return he started hanging around with another friend, Steve Wozniak, an electronics genius who'd built his own personal computer for fun but had little interest in selling it. Jobs had different ideas. Together they cofounded Apple Computer Inc. in Jobs's bedroom and soon they were assembling computers by hand in his parents' garage with some teenage friends. To fund their business, Jobs sold his Volkswagen microbus. Wozniak sold his calculator. Jobs was twenty-one; Wozniak, twenty-six.

Catching the tail of the early PC revolution, Apple took off like a rocket. It went public in 1980 with the biggest public offering since Ford Motor Company in 1956, making instant multimillionaires of those employees with stock options. In 1983, Apple entered the Fortune 500 at number 411, the fastest ascent of any company in business history. "I was worth about over a million dollars when I was twenty-three and over ten million dollars when I was twenty-four and over a hundred million dollars when I was twenty-five, and it wasn't that important because I never did it for the money," Jobs said.

Wozniak was the hardware genius, the chip-head engineer, but Jobs understood the whole package. Thanks to Jobs's ideas about design and advertising, the Apple II became the first successful mass-market computer for ordinary consumers—and turned Apple into the Microsoft of the early eighties. Bored, Jobs moved on to the Mac, the first commercial implementation of the revolutionary graphical user interface developed in computer research labs. Jobs didn't invent the graphical user interface that is used on almost every computer today, including millions of Bill Gates's Windows machines, but he brought it to the masses. This has been Jobs's stated goal from the very beginning: to create easy-to-use technology for the widest possible audience.

In 1985, Jobs was effectively kicked out of Apple for being unproductive and uncontrollable. After a failed power struggle with then-CEO John Sculley, Jobs quit before he could be fired. With dreams of revenge, he founded NeXT with the purpose of selling advanced computers to schools and putting Apple out of business. He also picked up a struggling computer graphics company for $10 million from *Star Wars* director George Lucas, who needed cash for a divorce. Renamed Pixar, Jobs propped up the struggling company for a decade with $60 million of his own money, only to see it eventually produce a string of block-busters and turn into Hollywood's premiere animation studio.

NeXT, on the other hand, never took off. In eight years it sold only 50,000 computers and had to exit the hardware business, concentrating on selling software to niche customers like the CIA. This is where Jobs could have disappeared from public life. With NeXT failing, Jobs might have written his memoirs or become a venture capitalist like many before him. But in hindsight, NeXT was a stunning success. NeXT's software was the impetus for Jobs's return to Apple, and it became the foundation of several key Apple technologies, especially Apple's highly regarded and influential Mac OS X.

Jobs's return to the company in 1996—the first time he set foot on the Cupertino campus in eleven years—has turned out to be the greatest comeback in business history. "Apple is engaged in probably the most remarkable second act ever seen in technology," Eric Schmidt, Google's chief executive, told *Time* magazine. "Its resurgence is simply phenomenal and extremely impressive."[6]

Jobs has made one savvy move after another. The iPod is a smash and the iPhone looks like one, too. Even the Mac, once written off as an expensive toy for a niche audience, is staging a roaring comeback. The Mac, like Apple itself, is now thoroughly mainstream. In ten years Jobs has hardly made a single mis-step, except one big one: he overlooked Napster and the digital music revolution in 2000. When customers wanted CD burners, Apple was making iMacs with DVD drives and promoting them as video editing machines. "I felt like a dope," he told *Fortune* magazine.[7]

Of course, it's not all been savvy planning. Jobs has been lucky. Early one morning in 2004, a scan revealed a cancerous tumor on his pancreas: a death sentence. Pancreatic cancer is a sure and quick killer. "My doctor advised me to go home and get my affairs in order, which is doctor's code for prepare to die," Jobs said. "It means to try to tell your kids everything you thought you'd have the next ten years to tell them in just a few months. It means to make sure everything is buttoned up so that it will be as easy as possible for your family. It means to say your goodbyes." But later that evening, a biopsy revealed that the tumor was an extremely rare form of cancer that is treatable with surgery. Jobs had the operation.[8]

Now in his early fifties, Jobs lives quietly, privately, with his wife and four kids in a large, unostentatious house in suburban Palo Alto. A Buddhist and a pescadarian (a vegetarian who eats fish), he often walks barefoot to the local Whole Foods for fruit or a smoothie. He works a lot, taking the occasional vacation in Hawaii. He draws $1 in salary from Apple but is getting rich (and ever richer) from share options—the same options that almost got him into trouble with the SEC—and he flies in a personal $90 million Gulfstream V jet granted to him by Apple's board.

These days, Jobs is in the zone. Apple is firing on all

cylinders, but its business model is thirty years out of date. Apple is an anomaly in an industry that long ago standardized on Microsoft. Apple should have gone to the big swap meet in the sky, like Osborne, Amiga, and a hundred other early computer companies that stuck to their own proprietary technology. But for the first time in a couple of decades, Apple is in a position to become a big, powerful, commercial presence—opening up new markets that are potentially much bigger than the computer industry it pioneered in the 1970s. There's a new frontier in technology: digital entertainment and communication.

The workplace was long ago revolutionized by computers, and Microsoft owns it. There's no way Apple is going to wrest control. But the home is a different matter. Entertainment and communication are going digital. People are communicating by cell phone, instant message, and e-mail, while music and movies are increasingly delivered online. Jobs is in a good position to sweep up. All the traits, all the instincts that made him a bad fit for the business world are perfect for the world of consumer devices. The obsession with industrial design, the mastery of advertising, and insistence on crafting seamless user experiences are key when selling high-tech to the masses.

Apple has become the perfect vehicle to realize Jobs's long-held dreams: developing easy-to-use technology for individuals. He's made—and remade—Apple in his own image. "Apple is Steve Jobs with ten thousand lives," Guy Kawasaki, Apple's former chief evangelist, told me.[9] Few corporations are such close mirror images of their founders. "Apple had always reflected the best and worst of Steve's character," said Gil Amelio, the CEO that Jobs replaced. "[Former CEOs] John Sculley, Michael Spindler, and I kept the place going but did not significantly alter the identity of the company. Though I have a lot to be angry about in my relationship with Steve Jobs, I recognize that much about the Apple I loved is tuned to his personality."[10]

Jobs runs Apple with a unique blend of uncompromising artistry and superb business chops. He's more of an artist than a businessman, but has the brilliant ability to capitalize on his creations. In some ways he's like Edwin Land, the scientist-industrialist who invented the Polaroid instant camera. Land is one of Jobs's heroes. Land made business decisions based on what was right as a scientist and as a supporter of civil and feminist rights, rather than a hardheaded businessman. Jobs also has in himself a bit of Henry Ford, another hero. Ford was a technology democratizer whose mass-production techniques brought automobiles to the masses. There's a streak of a modern-day Medici, a patron of the arts whose sponsorship of Jonathan Ive has ushered in a Renaissance for industrial design.

Jobs has taken his interests and personality traits—obsessiveness, narcissism, perfectionism—and turned them into the hallmarks of his career.

He's an elitist who thinks most people are bozos. But he makes gadgets so easy to use that a bozo can master them.

He's a mercurial obsessive with a filthy temper who has

forged a string of productive partnerships with creative, world-class collaborators: Steve Wozniak, Jonathan Ive, and Pixar director John Lasseter.

He's a cultural elitist who makes animated movies for kids; an aesthete and anti-materialist who pumps mass-market products out of Asian factories. He promotes them with an unrivaled mastery of the crassest medium, advertising.

He's an autocrat who has remade a big, dysfunctional corporation into a tight, disciplined ship that executes on his demanding product schedules.

Jobs has used his natural gifts and talents to remake Apple. He has fused high technology with design, branding, and fashion. Apple is less like a nerdy computer company than a brand-driven multinational like Nike or Sony: a unique blend of technology, design, and marketing.

His desire to craft complete customer experiences ensures Apple controls the hardware, the software, online services, and everything else. But it produces products that work seamlessly together and infrequently break down (even Microsoft, the epitome of the opposite approach, the open licensing model, is adopting the same modus operandi when selling Xbox game consoles and Zune music players to consumers).

Jobs's charm and charisma produce the best product introductions in the industry, a unique blend of theater and infomercial. His magnetic personality has also enabled him to negotiate superb contracts with Disney, the record labels, and AT&T—no pussycats when it comes to making deals. Disney gave him total creative freedom and a huge cut of profits at Pixar. The music labels helped turn the iTunes music store from an experiment into a threat. And AT&T signed up for the iPhone without even laying eyes on a prototype.

But where some see control freakery, others see a desire to craft a seamless, end-to-end user experience. Instead of perfectionism, there's the pursuit of excellence. And instead of screaming abuse, there's the passion to make a dent in the universe.

Here's someone who has turned his personality traits into a business philosophy.

Here's how he does it.

Chapter 1

Focus: How Saying "No" Saved Apple

"I'm looking for a fixer-upper with a solid foundation. Am willing to tear down walls, build bridges, and light fires. I have great experience, lots of energy, a bit of that 'vision thing' and I'm not afraid to start from the beginning."

—Steve Jobs's résumé at Apple's .Mac website

One bright July morning in 1997, Steve Jobs returned to the company he had cofounded twenty years before in his bedroom.

Apple was in a death spiral. The company was six months from bankruptcy. In just a couple of years, Apple had declined from one of the biggest computer companies in the world to an also-ran. It was bleeding cash and market share. No one was buying its computers, the stock was in the toilet, and the press was predicting its imminent passing.

Apple's top staff were summoned to an early-morning meeting at company HQ. In shuffled the then-current CEO, Gilbert Amelio, who'd been in charge for about eighteen months. He had patched up the company but had failed to re-ignite its inventive soul. "It's time for me to go," he said, and quietly left the room. Before anyone could react, Steve Jobs entered the room, looking like a bum. He was wearing shorts and sneakers and several days' worth of stubble. He plonked himself into a chair and slowly started to spin. "Tell me what's wrong with this place," he said. Before anyone could reply, he burst out: "It's the products. The products SUCK! There's no sex in them anymore."[1]

The Fall of Apple

Apple's fall was quick and dramatic. In 1994, Apple commanded nearly 10 percent of the worldwide multibillion-dollar market for personal computers. It was the second biggest computer manufacturer in the world after the giant IBM.[2] In 1995, Apple shipped the most computers it had ever sold—4.7 million Macs worldwide—but it wanted more. It wanted to be like Microsoft. It licensed the Macintosh operating system to several computer makers, including Power Computing, Motorola, Umax, and others. Apple's management reasoned that these "clone" machines would grow the overall Mac market. But it didn't work. The Mac market remained relatively flat, and the clone makers simply took sales away from Apple.

In the first quarter of 1996, Apple reported a loss of $69 million and laid off 1,300 staff. In February, the board fired CEO Michael Spindler and appointed in his place Gil Amelio, a veteran of the chip industry with a reputation as a turnaround artist. But in the eighteen months that Amelio was on the job, he proved ineffectual and unpopular. Apple lost $1.6 billion, its market share plummeted from 10 percent to 3 percent, and the stock collapsed. Amelio laid off thousands of workers, but he was raking in about $7 million in salary and benefits, and was sitting on $26 million in stock, according to the *New York Times*. He lavishly refurbished Apple's executive offices and, it was soon revealed, negotiated a golden parachute worth about $7 million. The *New York Times* called Amelio's Apple a "kleptocracy."[3]

But Amelio did several things right. He canceled a raft of money-losing projects and products, and trimmed the company to stem the losses. Most important, he bought Jobs's company, NeXT, hoping that its modern and robust operating system could replace the Macintosh operating system, which was becoming very creaky and old.

The NeXT purchase came about by accident. Amelio was interested in buying the BeOS, a fledgling operating system built by a former Apple executive, Jean Louis Gassée. But while they were haggling, Garret L. Rice, a NeXT salesman, called Apple out of the blue, suggesting they take a look. Apple's engineers hadn't even considered NeXT.

His interest piqued, Amelio asked Jobs to pitch the NeXT operating system.

In December 1996, Jobs gave Amelio an impressive demonstration of NeXT. Unlike the BeOS, NeXT was finished. Jobs had customers, developers, and hardware partners. NeXT also had a full suite of advanced and very highly regarded programming tools, which made it very easy for other companies to write software for it. "His people had spent a lot of time thinking about key issues like networking and the world of the internet—much more so than anything else around. Better than anything Apple had done, better than NT, and potentially better than what Sun had," Amelio wrote.[4]

During negotiations, Jobs was very low key. He didn't oversell. It was "a refreshingly honest approach, especially for Steve Jobs," Amelio said.[5] "I was relieved he wasn't coming on like a high-speed train. There were places in the presentation to think and question and discuss."

The pair hammered out the deal over a cup of tea in Jobs's kitchen at his house in Palo Alto. The first question was the price, which was based on the stock price. The second question concerned the stock options held by his NeXT employees. Amelio was impressed that he was watching out for his staff. Stock options have traditionally been one of the most important forms of compensation in Silicon Valley, and Jobs has used them many times to recruit and retain key staff, as discussed later in Chapter 5. But in November 2006, the SEC launched a probe into more than 130 companies, including Apple, that embroiled Jobs in accusations of improperly backdating options to inflate their worth. Jobs denied knowingly breaking the law, and the SEC investigation is still ongoing.

Jobs suggested they go for a walk, a surprise to Amelio but a standard Jobs tactic.

"I was hooked in by Steve's energy and enthusiasm," Amelio said. "I do remember how animated he is on his feet, how his full mental abilities materialize when he's up and moving, how he becomes more expressive. We headed back for the house with a deal wrapped up."[6]

Two weeks later, on December 20, 1996, Amelio announced that Apple was buying NeXT for $427 million. Jobs returned to Apple as a "special advisor" to Amelio, to help with the transition. It was the first time Jobs had been at the Apple campus in almost eleven years. Jobs had left Apple in 1985 after a failed power struggle with then-CEO John Sculley. Jobs had quit before he could be fired, and he had set up NeXT as a direct rival to Apple, hoping to run Apple out of business. Now he thought it might be too late to save Apple.

Enter the iCEO

At first Jobs was reluctant to take on a role at Apple. He was already CEO of another company—Pixar, which was just starting to take off with the enormous success of its first movie, *Toy Story*. With his success in Hollywood, Jobs was reluctant to get back into the technology business at Apple. Jobs was tiring of cranking out technology products that were quickly obsolete. He wanted to make things that were longer lasting. A good movie, for example. Good storytelling lasts for decades. In 1997, Jobs told *Time*:

"I don't think you'll be able to boot up any computer today in 20 years. [But] *Snow White* has sold 28 million copies, and it's a 60-year-old production. People don't read Herodotus or Homer to their kids anymore, but everybody watches movies. These are our myths today. Disney puts those myths into our culture, and hopefully Pixar will, too."[7]

Perhaps more important, Jobs was skeptical that Apple could stage a comeback. He was so skeptical, in fact, that in June 1997 he had sold the 1.5 million shares he'd received for the NeXT purchase at rock-bottom prices—all except for a single symbolic share. He didn't think Apple had a future worth more than one share.

But in early July 1997, Apple's board asked Amelio to resign following a string of terrible quarterly financial results, including one that resulted in a loss of three-quarters of a billion dollars, the biggest loss ever for a Silicon Valley company.[8]

The common perception is that Jobs ousted Amelio after backstabbing him in a carefully engineered boardroom coup. But there's no evidence to suggest that Jobs planned to take over the company. In fact, the opposite seems to be true. Several people interviewed for this book said Jobs initially had no interest whatsoever in returning to Apple—he was too busy with Pixar, and he had little confidence that Apple could be saved.

Even Amelio's own autobiography makes it clear that Jobs had no interest in taking the helm at Apple, if you ignore Amelio's assertions to the contrary. "He had never intended that the deal would include his giving Apple any more than some portion of his attention,"[9] Amelio wrote. Earlier in his book, Amelio noted that Jobs wanted to be paid in cash for the purchase of NeXT; he didn't want any Apple stock. But Amelio insisted on paying a large portion in shares because he didn't want Jobs walking away. He wanted Jobs committed to Apple, to have "some skin in the game," as he put it.[10]

Amelio does accuse Jobs several times of engineering his dismissal so that he, Jobs, could take over, but presents no direct evidence. It's more comforting for Amelio to blame his dismissal on maneuvering by Jobs than on the more straightforward explanation that Apple's board had lost confidence in him.

After firing Amelio, Apple's board had no one else to turn to. Jobs had already been dispensing advice to the company in his role as special advisor to Amelio (nothing particularly Machiavellian about that). The board asked Jobs to take over. He agreed to—temporarily. After six months, Jobs adopted the title of interim CEO, or iCEO, as he was jokingly referred to inside Apple. In August, Apple's board officially made Jobs the interim CEO while it continued to look for a permanent replacement. Wags noted that instead of Apple acquiring Jobs when it purchased NeXT, Jobs had acquired Apple but had cleverly arranged it so that Apple paid him.

When Jobs took over, Apple sold about forty different products—everything from inkjet printers to the Newton handheld. Few of them were market leaders. The lineup of computers was particularly baffling. There were several major lines—Quadras, Power Macs, Performas, and PowerBooks—each with a dozen different models. But there was little to distinguish between the models except their confusing product names—the Perfoma 5200CD, Perfoma 5210CD, Perfoma 5215CD, and Perfoma 5220CD.

"What I found when I got here was a zillion and one products," Jobs would later say. "It was amazing. And I started to ask people, now why would I recommend a 3400 over a 4400? When should somebody jump up to a 6500, but not a 7300? And after three weeks, I couldn't figure this out. If I couldn't figure this out ... how could our customers figure this out?"[11]

One engineer I interviewed who worked at Apple in the mid-1990s remembers seeing a poster-cum-flow-chart pinned to a wall at Apple's HQ. The poster was titled HOW TO CHOOSE YOUR MAC and was supposed to guide customers through the thicket of choices. But it merely illustrated how confused Apple's product strategy was. "You know something is wrong when you need a poster to choose your Mac," the engineer said.

Apple's organizational structure was in similar disarray.

Apple had grown into a big, bloated Fortune 500 company with thousands of engineers and even more managers. "Apple, pre Jobs, was brilliant, energetic, chaotic, and nonfunctional," recalled Don Norman, who was in charge of Apple's Advanced Technology Group when Jobs took over. Known as the ATG, the group was Apple's storied R&D division and had pioneered several important technologies.

"When I joined Apple in 1993 it was wonderful," he said to me in a telephone interview. "You could do creative, innovative things. But it was chaotic. You can't do that in an organization. You need a few creative people, and the rest get the work done."[12] According to Norman, Apple's engineers were rewarded for being imaginative and inventive, not for the difficult job of knuckling down and making things work. They would invent all day, but rarely did what they were told. As an executive, this would drive Norman crazy. Orders would be handed down, but incredibly, six months later nothing had happened. "It was ridiculous," Norman said.

John Warnock of Adobe, one of Apple's biggest software partners, said that changed quickly when Jobs returned. "He comes in with a very strong will and you sign up or get out of the way," Warnock said. "You have to run Apple that way— very direct, very forceful. You can't do it casually. When Steve attacks a problem, he attacks it with a vengeance. I think he mellowed during the NeXT years and he's not so mellow anymore."[13]

Steve's Survey

Within days of returning to Apple as the iCEO, Jobs got to work. Once he'd committed, Jobs was in a hurry to fix Apple. He immediately embarked on an extremely thorough survey of each and every product Apple made. He went through the company piece by piece, finding out what the assets were. "He needed to do a review of pretty much everything that was going on," said Jim Oliver, who was Jobs's assistant for several months after he returned to the company. "He talked to all the product groups. He wanted to know the scope and size of the research groups. He was saying, 'Everything needs to be justified. Do we really need a corporate library?' "

Jobs set up shop in a big conference room and called in the product teams one by one. As soon as everyone had convened, it went straight to work. "No introductions, absolutely not," Peter Hoddie recalled. Hoddie is a hotshot programmer who went on to become the chief architect of Apple's QuickTime multimedia software. "Someone started taking notes. Steve said: 'You don't need to take notes. If it's important, you'll remember it.' "

The engineers and programmers explained in detail what they were working on. They described their products in depth, explaining how they worked, how they were sold, and what they planned to do next. Jobs listened carefully and asked a lot of questions. He was deeply engaged. At the end of the presentations, he would sometimes ask hypothetical questions: "If money were no object, what would you do?"[14]

Jobs's review took several weeks. It was calm and methodical. There were none of the outbursts for which Jobs is infamous. "Steve said the company has to focus, and each individual group has to do the same," Oliver said. "It was quite formal. It was very calm. He'd say, 'Apple is in serious financial straits and we can't afford to do anything extra.' He was fairly gentle about it, but firm."

Jobs didn't cut from the top. He called on each product group to nominate what should be cut and what should be kept. If the group wanted to keep a project alive, it had to be sold to Jobs—and sold hard. Understandably, some of the teams argued to keep projects that were marginal, but were perhaps strategic, or the best technology on the market. But Jobs would frequently say that if it wasn't making a profit, it had to go. Oliver recalled that most of the teams volunteered a few sacrificial lambs to which Jobs responded, "It's not enough."

"If Apple is going to survive, we've got to cut more," Oliver recalled Jobs saying. "There were no screaming matches. There was no calling people idiots. It was simply, 'We've got to focus and do things we can be good at.'" Several times Oliver saw Jobs draw a simple chart of Apple's annual revenues on a whiteboard. The chart showed the sharp decline, from $12 billion a year to $10 billion, and then $7 billion. Jobs explained that Apple couldn't be a profitable $12 billion company, or a profitable

$10 billion company, but it could be a profitable $6 billion company.[15]

Apple's Assets

Over the next several weeks, Jobs made several important changes.

Senior Management. He replaced most of Apple's board with allies in the tech industry, including Oracle mogul Larry Ellison, who's also a friend. Several of Jobs's lieutenants from NeXT had already been given top positions at Apple: David Manovich was put in charge of sales; Jon Rubinstein, hardware; Avadis "Avie" Tevanian, software. Jobs set about replacing the rest of the executive staff, with one exception. He kept Fred Anderson, the chief financial officer, who had recently been hired by Amelio and wasn't considered old guard.

Microsoft. Jobs resolved a long-running and damaging patent lawsuit with Microsoft. In return for dropping charges that Microsoft ripped off the Mac in Windows, Jobs persuaded Gates to keep developing the all-important Office suite for the Mac. Without Office, the Mac was doomed. Jobs also got Gates to publicly support the company with a $150 million investment. The investment was largely symbolic, but Wall Street loved it: Apple stock shot up 30 percent. In return, Gates got

Jobs to make Microsoft's Internet Explorer the default web browser on the Mac, an important concession as Microsoft battled Netscape for control of the Web.

Jobs started talks with Gates personally, who then sent Microsoft's chief financial officer, Gregory Maffei, to hammer out a deal. Maffei went to Jobs's home and Jobs suggested they go for a walk around leafy Palo Alto. Jobs was barefoot. "It was a pretty radical change for the relations between the two companies," said Maffei. "[Jobs] was expansive and charming. He said, 'These are things that we care about and that matter.' And that let us cut down the list. We had spent a lot of time with Amelio, and they had a lot of ideas that were nonstarters. Jobs had a lot more ability. He didn't ask for 23,000 terms. He looked at the whole picture, figured out what he needed. And we figured he had the credibility to bring the Apple people around and sell the deal." [16]

The Brand. Jobs realized that while the products sucked, the Apple brand was still great. He considered the Apple brand as one of the core assets of the company, perhaps the core asset, but it needed to be revitalized. "What are the great brands? Levi's, Coke, Disney, Nike," Jobs told *Time* in 1998.[17] "Most people would put Apple in that category. You could spend billions of dollars building a brand not as good as Apple. Yet Apple hasn't been doing anything with this incredible asset. What is Apple, after all? Apple is about people who think outside the box, people who want to use computers to help them change the world, to help them create things that make a difference, and not just to get a job done."

Jobs held a "bake-off" between three top advertising agencies for Apple's account. He told them to pitch a big, bold rebranding campaign. The winner was TBWA/Chiat/Day, who had created Apple's legendary 1984 Super Bowl ad for the first Mac. As a result, TBWA created the "Think Different" campaign in close collaboration with Jobs. (More on "Think Different" in Chapter 4.)

The Customers. Jobs figured Apple's other major asset was its customers—about 25 million Mac users at the time. These were loyal customers, some of the most loyal customers of any corporation anywhere. If they continued to buy Apple's machines, they were a great foundation for a comeback.

The Clones. Jobs killed the clone business. The move was highly controversial, even inside the company, but it instantly allowed Apple to capture the whole Mac market again by eliminating the competition. Customers could no longer get a cheaper Mac from Power Computing or Motorola or Umax. The only competition was Windows, and Apple was a different proposition. Killing the clones was unpopular with Mac users who were becoming accustomed to buying cheap Macs from the clone makers, but the decision was the right strategic move for Apple.

The Suppliers. Jobs also negotiated new deals with Apple's suppliers. At the time, both IBM and Motorola were supplying Apple with chips. Jobs decided to pit them against each other. He told them that Apple was only going to go with one of them, and that he expected major concessions from the one he chose. He didn't drop either supplier, but because Apple was the only major customer of PowerPC chips from both companies, he got the concessions he wanted, and more important, guarantees of the chips' continued development. "It's like turning a big tanker," Jobs told *Time* magazine. "There were a lot of lousy deals that we're undoing."[18]

The Pipeline. The most important thing Jobs did was radically simplify Apple's product pipeline. In his modest office near the company's boardroom (he reportedly hated Amelio's refurbished offices and refused to occupy them), Jobs drew a very simple two-by-two grid on the whiteboard. Across the top he wrote "Consumer" and "Professional," and down the side, "Portable" and "Desktop." Here was Apple's new product strategy. Just four machines: two notebooks and two desktops, aimed at either consumers or professional users.

Slashing the product pipeline was an extremely gutsy move. It took a lot of nerve to cut a multibillion-dollar company back to the bone. To kill everything to focus on just four machines was radical. Some thought it was crazy, even suicidal. "Our jaws dropped when we heard that one," former Apple chairman Edgar Woolard Jr. told *Business Week*. "But it was brilliant."[19]

Jobs knew that Apple was only a few short months from bankruptcy, and the only way to save the company was to focus keenly on what it did best: build easy-to-use computers for consumers and creative professionals.

Jobs canceled hundreds of software projects and almost all the hardware. Amelio had already killed nearly three hundred projects at Apple—from prototype computers to new software—and laid off thousands of workers, but he had to stop there. "There's only so much cutting one CEO can do," Oliver said. "There was tremendous pressure on him when he did that. It made it much easier for Steve to take the fifty projects that remained and cut them back to ten."

Gone were the monitors, the printers, and—most controversially—the Newton handheld, a move that prompted Newton lovers to protest with placards and loudspeakers in Apple's parking lot. I GIVE A FIG FOR THE NEWTON, one placard read. NEWTON IS MY PILOT, said another.

The killing of the Newton was widely considered an act of vengeance on a previous Apple CEO, John Sculley, who had ousted Jobs from Apple in the late 1980s. The Newton was Sculley's baby, and here was Jobs knifing it to get revenge. After all, the Newton Division had just turned its first profit and was about to be spun off into a separate company. A whole new industry for handhelds was springing up, which would soon come to be dominated by the Palm Pilot.

But to Jobs, the Newton was a distraction. Apple was in the

computer business, and that meant it had to focus on computers. It was the same with laser printers. Apple was one of the first companies in the laser printer business and had carved out a big chunk of the market. Many thought Jobs was leaving millions of dollars on the table by getting out of it.

But Jobs argued that Apple should be selling premium computers: well-designed, well-made machines for the top end of the market, like luxury cars. Jobs would argue that all cars did the same thing—they went from A to B—but lots of people paid top dollar for a BMW over a Chevy. Jobs acknowledged that the analogy wasn't perfect (cars run on anyone's gas, but Macs couldn't run Windows software) but argued Apple's customer base was big enough to earn Apple good margins.

To Jobs, this was a key point. There was—and always has been—pressure on Apple to sell dirt-cheap computers. But Jobs insisted that Apple would never compete in the commodity computer market, which is a race to the bottom. Between Dell, Compaq, and Gateway, there were half a dozen computer makers, all making essentially the same product, distinguished only by price. Instead of taking on Dell with the cheapest possible computer, Apple would make first-class products to make enough profit to keep developing more first-class products. Volume would drive down the prices.

Cutting back the number of products was a good move operationally. Fewer products meant less inventory, which had an immediate impact on the company's bottom line. Jobs was able to cut Apple's inventory from more than $400 million to less than $100 million in one year.[20] Previously, the company had been forced to take write-downs of millions of dollars in unsold machines. By cutting the products back to a minimum, Jobs minimized the risk of getting hit with expensive writeoffs, the kind of hit that might have sunk the company.

The cutbacks and reorganization weren't easy on Jobs, who put in long, grueling hours. "I'd never been so tired in my life," Jobs told *Fortune* in 1998. "I'd come home at about ten o'clock at night and flop straight into bed, then haul myself out at six the next morning and take a shower and go to work. My wife deserves all the credit for keeping me at it. She supported me and kept the family together with a husband in absentia."[21]

He sometimes wondered if he was doing the right thing. He was already CEO of Pixar, which was enjoying the success of *Toy Story*. He knew that returning to Apple would put pressure on Pixar, his family, and his reputation. "I wouldn't be honest if some days I didn't question whether I made the right decision in getting involved," he told *Time*.[22] "But I believe life is an intelligent thing—that things aren't random."

Jobs was mostly worried about failing. Apple was in dire trouble, and he might not be able to save it. He'd already earned a place in the history books; now he didn't want to wreck it. In the 1998 interview with *Fortune*, Jobs said that he looked to his hero Bob Dylan for inspiration. One of the things that Jobs admired about Dylan was his refusal to stand still. Many successful artists at some point in their careers atrophy: they keep doing what made them successful in the first place, but they don't evolve. "If they keep on risking failure, they're still artists," Jobs said. "Dylan and Picasso were always risking failure."

Getting "Steved"

Even though there are no published reports of mass layoffs involving thousands of staff after Jobs took the helm, there were, in fact, mass layoffs. Most, if not all, were performed by the product managers, who laid off staff after projects were killed. But it was very quietly kept out of the papers.

There are stories—likely apocryphal—of Jobs cornering luckless employees in elevators and quizzing them on their role at the company. If the answers weren't satisfactory, they'd be fired on the spot. The practice became known as getting "steved." The term is now part of tech jargon for any project that gets unceremoniously terminated: "My online knitting pattern generator got steved."

Jim Oliver is doubtful that any employees were personally "steved" in elevators. Jobs may have fired someone on the spot, but it wasn't in Oliver's presence—and he accompanied Jobs almost everywhere for three months as his personal assistant. If Jobs did fire anyone, Oliver doubts he did it more than once. "But the stories certainly got around and put people on their toes," Oliver said. "These stories get repeated, but I never found the person he did it to."[23]

Based on what he'd heard, Oliver expected Jobs to be an unpredictable, bad-tempered basket case, and was pleasantly surprised to find him quite calm. Jobs's outbursts are overplayed, Oliver said. He did witness a few temper flare-ups but they were "very rare" and often premeditated. "The public dressing-downs were clearly calculated," Oliver said. (Jobs does have a tendency to polarize things, though. He has a certain favorite Pilot pen and all the others are "crap." People are either geniuses or bozos.)

Jobs may have killed the Newton, but he kept most of the Newton team, whom he had judged to be good engineers. He needed them to build one of the machines in his simplified product matrix: the consumer portable, later named the iBook. While doing his product survey, Jobs had also been conducting a people survey. The company's assets weren't just products, they were the employees as well. And there were some gems. "I found ten months ago the best industrial design team I've ever seen in my life," Jobs would later say, referring to Jonathan Ive and his team of designers. Ive was already working for Apple—he'd been at Apple for several years and had risen to head the design group. (Ive is detailed later, in Chapter 3.)

Jobs paid careful attention to find the talent on the product teams, even if they weren't the ones running the show. Peter Hoddie said that after the QuickTime presentation, in which he'd talked a lot about the software, Jobs asked him his name. "I didn't know if that was good or bad," Hoddie recalled. "But he remembered my name." Later, Hoddie became QuickTime's senior architect.

Jobs's plan was simple: cut back so that the core A team—his cadre of ex-NeXT execs, and the company's best programmers, engineers, designers, and marketers—could again develop innovative products, and keep improving and updating them. "If we could make four great product platforms that's all we need," Jobs explained in a 1998 interview. "We can put our A team on every single one of them instead of having a B or a C team on any. We can turn them much faster."[24] As we'll see in a later chapter, one of Jobs's key business strategies throughout his career has been to recruit the most talented people he can find.

Jobs made sure that Apple's organizational chart was streamlined and straightforward. His new managerial flowchart was pretty simple: Jon Rubinstein ran engineering, Avie Tevanian ran software, Jonathan Ive headed up the design group, Tim Cook ran operations, and Mitch Mandich ran worldwide sales. Jobs insisted on a clear chain of command all the way down the line: everyone in the company knew whom they reported to and what was expected of them. "The organization is clean and simple to understand, and very accountable," Jobs told *Business Week*.[25] "Everything just got simpler. That's been one of my mantras—focus and simplicity."

Dr. No

Jobs's dramatic focusing worked. Over the next two years, Apple introduced four machines that proved to be a string of hits.

First there was the Power Macintosh G3, a speedy professional machine introduced in November 1997. It's largely forgotten now, but the G3 was a big hit with Apple's core audience—professional users—and sold a very respectable one million units in its first year. The G3 was followed by the multicolored iBook and the sleek titanium PowerBook, which were both chart toppers. But it was the iMac, a fruity-colored teardrop-shaped machine, that was a blockbuster. The iMac sold six million units, becoming the best-selling computer of all time. The iMac became a cultural phenomenon, launching a dizzying array of see-through plastic products, from toothbrushes to hair dryers. Bill Gates was mystified by the iMac's success. "The one thing Apple's providing now is leadership in colors," he said. "It won't take long for us to catch up with that, I don't think."[26] Gates couldn't see that beyond the iMac's unusual colors, the computer had other merits that would make it a hit with consumers: easy setup, friendly software, and a distinct personality.

Jobs focused Apple on a small selection of products it could execute well. But that focus has also been applied to the individual products themselves. To avoid "feature creep"—the growing list of features that is often added to new products during their design stage and after their initial release—Jobs insists on a tight focus. Many cell phones are shining examples of feature creep. They do everything under the sun, but basic functions like adjusting the volume or checking voicemail are sometimes obscured by the devices' overwhelming complexity. To avoid confusing the consumer with an endless array of complex choices, one of Jobs's favorite mantras at Apple is: "Focus means saying no."

Focus is also having the confidence to say no when everyone else is saying yes. When Jobs launched the iMac, for example, it didn't have a floppy drive, then standard equipment on computers. It seems silly now, but there were howls of protest from customers and the press. Many pundits said the lack of a floppy drive was a fatal mistake that would doom the iMac. "The iMac is clean, elegant, floppy-free—and doomed," wrote Hiawatha Bray in the *Boston Globe* in May 1998.[27]

Jobs wasn't 100 percent sure of the decision himself, said Hoddie, but he trusted his gut that the floppy was becoming obsolete. The iMac was designed as an Internet computer, and owners would use the Net to transfer files or download software, Jobs reasoned. The iMac was also one of the first computers on the market to use USB, a new standard for connecting peripherals that no one except Intel was using (and Intel invented it). But the decision to ditch floppies and use USB put a forward-looking shine on the iMac. It seemed like a futuristic product, whether or not that was the intention.

Jobs also keeps Apple's product lineup very simple and focused. Throughout the late 1990s and early 2000s, Apple fielded at most half a dozen major product lines: two major desktop and laptop computers, some monitors, the iPod, and iTunes. Later, it added the Mac mini, the iPhone, the AppleTV, and some iPod accessories, like woolly socks and armbands. Contrast Jobs's insistence on maintaining a tight focus with other companies in the tech industry, especially the giants, like Samsung or Sony, which carpet bomb the market with hundreds of different products. Over the years, Sony has sold six hundred different models of the Walkman. Sony's CEO, Sir Howard Stringer, has expressed envy of companies with a narrow product lineup. "Sometimes I wish there were just three products," he has lamented.[28]

Sony can't release a product—any product—without multiple models at launch. This is usually perceived as good for customers. Conventional wisdom holds that more choice is always a good thing. But each variation costs the company time, energy, and resources. While a giant like Sony might have the means, Apple needed to focus and limit the number of variations it released just to get anything out the door.

Of course, with the iPod, Apple now has a Sony-like lineup of products. There are more than half a dozen different models, from the bare-bones Shuffle to the high-end video iPod and the iPhone, priced at every $50 price point between $100 and $350. But to get there took Apple several years—not all at launch.

Personal Focus

At a personal level, Jobs focuses on his areas of expertise and delegates all else. At Apple, he is very hands-on in areas he knows well: developing new products, overseeing marketing, and giving keynote speeches. At Pixar, Jobs was just the opposite. He delegated the moviemaking process to his capable lieutenants. Jobs's main role at Pixar was cutting deals with Hollywood, a skill at which he excels. Let's break down these areas this way.

What Jobs is good at:

1. **Developing new products.**

   Jobs is a master at conceiving and helping to create innovative new products. From the Mac to the iPod and the iPhone, Jobs's passion is for inventing new products.

2. **Product presentations.**

   Steve Jobs is the public face of Apple. When the company has a new product, Jobs is the one who introduces it to the world. For this he spends weeks in preparation.

3. **Cutting deals.**

   Jobs is a master negotiator. He cut great deals with Disney to distribute Pixar's movies and persuaded all five major record labels to sell music through iTunes.

What Jobs is NOT good at:

1. Directing movies.

At Apple, Jobs has a reputation as a micromanager and a meddler, but at Pixar, he was very hands-off. Jobs can't direct movies, so he doesn't even try. (More on Pixar in Chapter 4.)

2. Dealing with Wall Street.

Jobs has little interest in dealing with Wall Street. For many years, he trusted the company's financials to his CFO, Fred Anderson. Until Apple's stock options scandal in 2006 and 2007, Anderson was widely admired and respected for his handling of the company's financials.

3. Operations.

Likewise, Jobs delegates the tricky job of operations to his veteran COO, Tim Cook, who is widely regarded as his right-hand man. (When Jobs was treated for cancer, Cook took over as temporary CEO.) Under Cook, Apple has become an extremely lean and efficient operation. Jobs boasts that Apple is more efficient than Dell, supposedly the industry's operational gold standard. (More on this in Chapter 6.)

4. Staying focused.

Over the years, the list of products Jobs hasn't done has grown quite long: from handhelds to web tablets and low-end, bare-bones computers. "We look at a lot of things, but I'm as proud of the products that we have not done as I am of the ones we have done," Jobs told the *Wall Street Journal*.[29]

Apple's labs are littered with prototype products that never made it out the door. The product Jobs is most proud of not doing is a PDA, a personal digital assistant, the successor to the Newton he discontinued in 1998. Jobs has admitted he's done a lot of *thinking* about a PDA, but by the time Apple was ready—in the early 2000s—he'd decided the PDA's time had already passed. PDAs were fast being superseded by cell phones with address books and calendar functions. "We got enormous pressure to do a PDA and we looked at it and we said, 'Wait a minute, 90 percent of the people that use these things just want to get information out of them, they don't necessarily want to put information into them on a regular basis and cellphones are going to do that,'" Jobs told the *Wall Street Journal*.[30] He was right: witness the iPhone. (And the Palm, which hasn't adapted well, is now on the ropes.)

There have also been calls for Apple to sell to big business, the so-called enterprise market. Jobs has resisted because selling to companies—no matter how big the potential market—is outside of Apple's focus. Since Jobs's return, Apple has focused on consumers. "The roots of Apple were to build computers for people, not for corporations," Jobs has said. "The world doesn't need another Dell or Compaq."[31]

There are much greater profits to be made selling a $3,000 machine than a $500 machine, even if you sell fewer of them. By aiming at the middle and high end of the market, Apple enjoys some of the best profit margins in the business: about 25 percent. Dell's profit margins are only about 6.5 percent, while Hewlett-Packard's are even lower, about 5 percent.

In the summer of 2007, Dell was the biggest PC manufacturer in the world, with a whopping 30 percent share of the U.S. market. Apple trailed third, with a much smaller 6.3 percent market share.[32] But in the third quarter of 2007, Apple reported a record profit of $818 million, while Dell, which sells more than *five times* as many machines, earned only $2.8 million in profit. Yes, a big chunk of Apple's profit came from the sale of iPods, and Dell was going through a restructuring, but Apple clearly makes much more money on the sale of a $3,500 high-end MacBook Pro laptop (as much as $875) than Dell makes on a $500 system (about $25). This is why Dell bought Alienware, a boutique gaming machine manufacturer, in 2006.

It's been clear for years that Apple doesn't compete in the same market as PC companies, but for many years its health as a business was measured by the number of machines it sold, not the value of those machines. Success in the PC market has traditionally been measured by quantity, not quality. Pundits and industry-watch Gartner Inc. made repeated calls for Apple to exit the hardware business because its market share in the 2000s slipped into low single digits. But Apple goes after the most profitable segment of the market, not the most number of machines, although this is starting to change.

Lessons from Steve

- *Get busy.* Roll up your sleeves and get to work straight away.
- *Face hard decisions head-on.* Jobs has to make some hard, painful decisions, but faces the situation head-on.
- *Don't get emotional.* Assess your company's problems with a cool, clear head.
- *Be firm.* It couldn't have been easy, but Jobs was firm and fair when he stepped back into Apple and began his drastic reorganization. He knew what had to be done. He took the time to explain it, and he expected the staff to fall in line.
- *Get informed; don't guess.* Make a thorough inspection of the company and base your decisions on data, not hunches. It's tough but fair.
- *Reach out for help.* Don't shoulder the burden alone. Jobs asks for the company's help, and he gets it. The managers help shoulder the burden of any cuts.
- *Focus means saying "no."* Jobs focuses Apple's limited resources on a small number of projects it can execute well.
- *Stay focused; don't allow feature creep.* Keep things simple, which is a virtue in a world of overly complex technology.
- *Focus on what you are good at; delegate all else.* Jobs doesn't direct animated movies or woo Wall Street. He concentrates on what he's good at.

Chapter 2

Despotism: Apple's One-Man Focus Group

"We made the buttons on the screen look so good you'll want to lick them."

—Steve Jobs, on Mac OS X's user interface, *Fortune*, January 24, 2000

Before Jobs returned to Apple, the company had spent several years fruitlessly trying to develop a modern version of the Macintosh operating system. Since its debut in 1984, the old Mac OS had turned into a bloated, unstable patchwork of code. It had become a nightmare to maintain and upgrade. For users, it meant constant crashes, freezes, and restarts—and lots of lost data, frustration, and rage.

Because large portions of the Mac OS were still based on creaky old code, Apple decided that it had to start from scratch. In 1994, programmers began a ground-up rewrite of the operating system, code-named Copland, after the famous American composer. But after a couple of years of effort, it became apparent the project was a gargantuan effort and would never be finished. The Apple executive team at the time decided it would be easier (and wiser) to purchase a next-generation operating system from another company rather than develop one itself. The search eventually led to the purchase of Steve Jobs's NeXT.

Apple was interested in NeXTstep, a surprisingly advanced and sophisticated operating system that Jobs had developed during his wilderness years away from Apple. NeXTstep had everything the old Mac OS lacked. It was fast, stable, and almost crash-proof. It had modern networking features—essential in the Internet age—and a modular architecture that was easily modified and upgraded. It also came with a collection of great programming tools, which made it very easy for software developers to write programs for it. Programming tools are a huge competitive advantage in the tech industry. Computer platforms are doomed unless they can attract talented programmers to create applications for them, just like game consoles are doomed unless they can attract great games. From the Mac to the Palm Pilot and the Xbox, the success of a platform is primarily determined by the software that can run on it. In some cases this is the so-called killer app—an essential piece of software that guarantees the success of the platform, like Office on Windows, or the game Halo on the Xbox.

What's NeXT?

After buying NeXT, Apple had to figure out how to turn NeXT-step into a Macintosh operating system. At first, the job looked so big that Apple's programmers decided they should take the old interface in Mac OS 8 and try to graft it on top of the NeXT-step codebase. According to Cordell Ratzlaff, the manager who was charged with overseeing the job, the interface graft didn't look like it would present much of a challenge. "We assigned one designer to OS X," he recalled. "His job was pretty boring: make the new stuff look like the old stuff."

But Ratzlaff thought it was a shame to put an ugly façade on such an elegant system, and he soon had designers creating mockups of new interface designs. Ratzlaff told me that the mockups were designed to show off many of the advanced technologies under NeXTstep's hood—especially its powerful graphics and animation capabilities.[1]

Ratzlaff, a soft-spoken creative director for Frog Design, a storied and internationally famous design company, worked at Apple for nine years. Starting as a designer, he rose through the ranks to lead the human interface group for Mac OS. In this role, Ratzlaff was in charge of the look and feel of Apple's operating systems from Mac OS 8 through the first release of OS X.

Interfaces these days are colorful and dynamic, but in the late 1990s, both Apple's and Microsoft's operating systems were plain and gray, with boxy windows, sharp corners, and lots of bevels. Then Apple came out with the tear-shaped iMac, a computer with a transparent plastic shell and curvy organic lines. It was a big inspiration to Ratzlaff and his colleagues. They soon had mockups of colorful, airy interfaces with see-through menus, soft edges, and round, organic buttons.

Ratzlaff's boss, Bertrand Serlet, now Apple's senior vice president of software engineering, admired the mockups but he made it clear there was neither the time nor resources to implement them. OS X's lone designer continued to graft the old Mac interface onto NeXTstep.

After several months of work, Apple held an off-site for all the engineering groups working on OS X to gather a status report. Ratzlaff was asked to show his mockups, mostly just for kicks. His talk would be some light relief at the end of a long, hard week. He was scheduled as the last speaker on the last day. But he secretly hoped there'd be support for the new designs and they'd be implemented, although he didn't rate his chances. As the two-day event wore on, it became clearer and clearer what an enormous project OS X was. Everyone was wondering how it was ever going to get done. "And then here at the end, here's me saying, 'Oh, and here's a new user interface. It's translucent, there's real-time animation, and a full alpha channel,'" Ratzlaff recalled. "There was literally laughter in the room because there was no way we were going to redo the user interface. I was pretty depressed afterwards."

"You're a Bunch of Idiots"

Two weeks later Ratzlaff got a call from Steve Jobs's assistant. Jobs hadn't seen the mockups at the off-site—he hadn't attended—but now he wanted a peek. At the time, Jobs was still conducting his survey of all the product groups. Ratzlaff and his designers were sitting in a conference room waiting for Jobs, when he walked in and immediately called them "a bunch of amateurs."

"You're the guys who designed Mac OS, right?" he asked them. They sheepishly nodded yes. "Well, you're a bunch of idiots."

Jobs rattled off all the things he hated about the old Mac interface, which was just about everything. One of the things he hated most were all the different mechanisms for opening windows and folders. There were at least eight different ways of accessing folders—from dropdown menus to pop-up menus, the DragStrip, the Launcher, and the Finder. "The trouble was, you had too many windows," said Ratzlaff. "Steve wanted to simplify window management." Because Ratzlaff was the one primarily responsible for these features, he started to get nervous about his job, but after twenty minutes of withering criticism, Ratzlaff realized his position was probably safe. "I figure he's not going to fire us, because that would've happened already," Ratzlaff said.

Jobs, Ratzlaff, and the designers settled into an in-depth discussion of the old Mac interface and how it might be overhauled. Ratzlaff's team showed Jobs their mockups and the meeting wrapped up well. "Prototype these things and show them to me," Jobs instructed them.

The design team worked for three weeks, night and day, building working prototypes in Macromedia Director, a multimedia authoring tool often used for mocking up custom interfaces for software or websites. "We knew our jobs were on the line so we were pretty worried," he said. "He [Jobs] came over to the offices. We spent the whole afternoon with him. He was blown away. From that point on, it was clear there was going to be a new user interface for OS X."

Jobs was so impressed that he said to Ratzlaff: "This is the first evidence of three-digit intelligence at Apple I've seen yet." Ratzlaff was happy to take the compliment. For Jobs, acknowledging you have an IQ higher than 100 is a glowing endorsement. Confident that their jobs were safe, Ratzlaff and the designers celebrated with a few six-packs of beer. But they became nervous when they saw Jobs coming back down the corridor with Phil Schiller, Apple's head of marketing. Luckily, Jobs was pleased. As Jobs approached, they heard him tell Schiller excitedly, "You've got to see this."

"From then on we had no trouble," Ratzlaff said.

No Detail Too Small

For the next eighteen months, Ratzlaff's team had a weekly meeting with Jobs during which they'd show him their latest mockups. For each element of the new interface—the menus, the dialogs, the radio buttons—Jobs requested several variations so that he could select the best ones. As we'll see in more detail later, Jobs always asks for multiple variations of products in development—both hardware and software. During the meetings with Ratzlaff, Jobs gave lots of feedback for refining the designs, and only when he was satisfied could features be ticked off.

The design team's mockups, in Macromedia Director, were dynamic, but they weren't functioning software. Jobs could open and close windows, pull down menus, and see how the system would work. But they were only animations. They weren't working code. The team had the working code running on another machine that was placed next to the Director demo. When they showed the working code to Jobs, he'd lean forward, his nose to the screen, and examine them closely, moving from the demo to the prototype and back again.

"He would compare them pixel by pixel to see if they matched," Ratzlaff said. "He was way down into the details. He would scrutinize everything, down to the pixel level." If they didn't match, Ratzlaff said, "some engineer would get yelled at."

Incredibly, Ratzlaff's team spent six months refining the scrollbars to Jobs's satisfaction. Scrollbars are an important part of any computer operating system but are hardly the most visible element of the user interface. Nonetheless, Jobs insisted the scrollbars look just so, and Ratzlaff's team had to design version after version. "It had to be done right," said Ratzlaff, laughing at the effort that went into such a seemingly minor detail.

At first, the design team found it very difficult to get the scrollbar details true. The little arrows were the wrong size, or in the wrong place, or the color was off. The scrollbars had to look different if the window was the currently active window or one of the background windows. "It was pretty hard to get them to fit with the rest of the design in all these different states," Ratzlaff said with a note of weariness in his voice. "We kept at it until it was right. We worked on it for a long, long time."

Simplifying the UI

OS X's interface was designed with new users in mind. Because the system would be new to everyone—even veteran Mac users—Jobs focused on simplifying the interface as much as possible. For example, in the old Mac OS, most of the settings that determined system behavior were hidden away in myriad System Extensions, Control Panel menus, and special dialog boxes of the various system components. Setting up an Internet connection used to involve tweaking settings in up to half a dozen different places.

To simplify things, Jobs ordered as many settings as possible to be collected together into a single System Preferences box that lived in a new navigation element called "The Dock."

The Dock is an icon-filled bar that sits at the bottom of the screen. It is home to commonly used applications and the system trashcan. It can accommodate all kinds of stuff, from frequently used folders to mini-programs called "scripts."

Jobs insisted on stripping back as many interface elements as possible, maintaining that the content of the windows were the most important thing, not the windows themselves. His desire to strip back and simplify put an end to several major features, including a single-window mode that the design team worked on for many months.

Jobs hated having multiple windows open. Every time a new folder or document was opened, it spawned a new window. Quickly, the screen was filled with overlapping windows. So the designers created a special single-window mode. Everything was displayed in the same window, no matter which software program the user was working in. The window would display a spreadsheet, then a text document or a digital photo. The effect was rather like jumping from website to website in a single web browser window, except here it was between documents stored on the local hard drive.

Sometimes the system worked well, but the window often had to be resized to display different kinds of documents. When working with a text document, the window was best made thin and narrow to make it easy to scroll up and down the text. But if the user opened an image in landscape format, the window would have to be widened.

But this wasn't the biggest problem. Critically for Jobs, the system required the designers to create a dedicated button in the window toolbar to switch it on and off. Jobs decided, in the interest of simplicity, to take the button away. He could live with resizing windows, but not the additional button cluttering the menu bar. "The extra button wasn't justified by the functionality," Ratzlaff said.

While working on the new interface, Jobs would sometimes suggest what at first seemed to be crazy ideas, but later turned out to be good ones. At one meeting, he was scrutinizing the three tiny buttons in the top left corner of every window. The three buttons were for closing, shrinking, and expanding the window, respectively. The designers had made all the buttons the same muted gray, to prevent them from distracting the user, but it was difficult to tell what the buttons were for. It was suggested that their functions should be illustrated by an animation that was triggered when the mouse cursor hovered over them.

But then Jobs made what seemed like an odd suggestion: that the buttons should be colored like traffic stoplights: red to close the window, yellow to shrink it, and green to expand it. "When we heard that, we felt that was a strange thing to associate with a computer," Ratzlaff said. "But we worked on it for a little while and he was right." The color of the button implicitly suggested the consequence of clicking it, especially the red button, which suggested "danger" if the user clicked it but didn't mean to close the window.

Introducing OS X

Jobs knew that OS X would cause a huge outcry from Apple's outside software developers, who would have to rewrite all their software to run on the new system. Even with OS X's great programming tools, there would be pushback from developers. Jobs and his executives struggled with the best way to approach the software community. Eventually they came up with a strategy: if they could persuade just three of the biggest companies to embrace OS X, everyone else would follow. The big three were Microsoft, Adobe, and Macromedia.

It worked—eventually. Microsoft supported OS X from the get-go, thanks to Jobs's 1998 deal with Bill Gates that cemented five years of software support. But Adobe and Macromedia weren't so quick to convert their big applications like Photoshop and Dreamweaver. Both companies eventually ported them over, but they refused to rewrite their consumer applications for OS X, a decision that led Apple to develop its own application software and, indirectly, the iPod (more on this later).

While it was no secret Apple was working on OS X, the fact that it had a new interface was. The interface was designed in intense secrecy. Very few people at Apple even knew the interface was being overhauled, only the handful of people working on it. One of Jobs's stated rationales for keeping it secret was to prevent others—Microsoft in particular—from copying it.

But more important, Jobs didn't want to kill sales of the current Macintosh operating system. Jobs wanted to avoid what's known as the Osborne effect, where a company commits suicide by announcing cool technology still under development.

As soon as OS X development started, Jobs directed everyone at Apple to stop criticizing the current Mac OS in public. For years, Apple's programmers had been quite frank about the system's problems and shortcomings. "Mac OS X was his baby, so he knew how great it was," said Peter Hoddie. "But he said for the next few years we've got to focus on Mac OS because we'll never get there without it. He was like Khrushchev, banging his shoe on the table. 'You've got to support the Mac OS, kids. Get this through your heads.' "[2]

Jobs unveiled Mac OS X in January 2000 at Macworld, after nearly two and a half years of work by nearly one thousand programmers. Mac OS X was a colossal undertaking. It was—and arguably still is—the most sophisticated computer interface designed to date, with complex, real-time graphics effects like transparency, shadowing, and animation. But it had to run on every G3 processor Apple had on the market, and it had to run in as little as 8 Mbytes of video memory. It was a very tall order.

While introducing OS X at Macworld, Jobs also announced that he was becoming Apple's permanent CEO, which drew huge applause from the keynote crowd. Several Apple employees have noted that Jobs didn't become the company's permanent CEO until after OS X shipped in March 2001. By this point, Jobs had been at Apple's helm for two and a half years, and had replaced almost all the directors and senior staff, fixed marketing and advertising, reinvigorated hardware with the iMac, and reorganized sales. Ratzlaff noted that with OS X, Jobs had overhauled the company and all of Apple's major products. "He was waiting for the last big parts of the company to be running to his standards before he took on the role of Apple CEO," said Ratzlaff.

Jobs's Design Process

For many years, Apple encouraged strict adherence to its Human Interface Guidelines, a standards bible designed to ensure a consistent user experience across software applications. The HIG told designers where to put menus, what kind of commands they should contain, and how to design dialog boxes. The idea was that all Mac software would behave alike, no matter which company it came from.

The guidelines were first drafted in the 1980s, when computers were used primarily to produce things, such as creating and printing out documents. But in the Internet age, computers are used for communication and media consumption as much as they are for printing documents and editing video. Software for playing movies or videoconferencing with friends can be much simpler than applications like Photoshop or Excel. Often, only a few functions are required, and all the drop-down menus and dialog boxes can be jettisoned in favor of a few simple buttons. In the late 1990s and early 2000s, there was a steady shift toward single-purpose mini-applications in both Mac (Widgets) and Windows (Gadgets).

Apple's QuickTime player was an early example of software that benefited from an interface rethink. Used to play multimedia files, mostly music and video, the player needed only a few controls for starting and pausing movies and adjusting the sound. It was decided that the QuickTime player should be one of the first pieces of Apple's software to get a simple appliance-like interface.

The player's interface was designed by Tim Wasko, a soft-spoken Canadian who later went on to design the iPod interface. Wasko came to Apple from NeXT, where he'd worked with Jobs. Wasko is known at Apple as a design god. "He's a total fiend at Photoshop," said Hoddie. "You'd say, 'What about this idea?' and it'd be: click click, click"—Hoddie mimicked the sound of fingers flying across a keyboard—"and it was rendered already."

The QuickTime player design team was made up of half a dozen designers and programmers, including Hoddie and Wasko. They met with Jobs once or twice a week over six months. Each week, the team would present a dozen or more new designs, often playing around with different textures and looks. Early ideas included a yellow plastic motif inspired by Sony's Sport Walkman, and various wood or metal textures. Anything was game. "Steve is not a design radical, but he is willing to try new things," said Hoddie.

At first, the designs were presented on a computer, but the team found that flashing them on and off screen was a laborious process, so they switched to printing out the designs on large glossy sheets of paper. The printouts were spread over a large conference table and could be quickly sorted through. Jobs and the designers found it easy to pick out the designs they liked from the pile, saying this texture should go with that shape. The method proved to be so effective that most of Apple's designers have since adopted it.

After the meetings, Jobs would sometimes take away a handful of printouts and show them to other people. "He has great design sense, but he's also listening," said Hoddie.

After several weeks of playing around with different designs, Wasko came up with a metallic look, which Jobs liked but thought wasn't quite right. At the next meeting Jobs showed up with a brochure from Hewlett-Packard with the HP logo in brushed metal, resembling a high-end kitchen appliance. "I like this one," Jobs told the group. "See what you can do."

The team came back with a brushed-metal look for the QuickTime player, which for several years since became the predominant design motif used extensively across Apple's software plus its high-end hardware. Through the early 2000s, most of Apple's applications were given a brushed-metal look, from the Safari web browser to the iCal calendar.

Jobs is intimately involved in the design process. He brings a lot of ideas to the table and always makes suggestions for improving designs. Jobs's contribution is not just choosing what he likes and dislikes. "He's not, 'this is bad, this is good,'" said Hoddie. "He's really part of the design."

Deceptive Simplicity

Jobs is never interested in technology for technology's sake. He never loads up on bells and whistles, cramming features into a product simply because they're easy to add. Just the opposite. Jobs pares back the complexity of his products until they are as simple and easy to use as possible. Lots of Apple's products are designed from the user's point of view.

Take the iTunes online music store, which launched in 2001, at the height of the popularity of online file sharing. A lot of people asked at the time how the store would compete with piracy. Why would anyone spend $1 a song, when they could get the same song for free? Jobs's answer was the "customer experience." Instead of wasting time on the file-sharing networks, trying to find songs, music fans could log on to iTunes and buy songs with a single click. They're guaranteed quality and reliability, with the ease of one-click shopping. "We don't see how you convince people to stop being thieves, unless you can offer them a carrot—not just a stick," Jobs said. "And the carrot is: We're gonna offer you a better experience ... and it's only gonna cost you a dollar a song."[3]

Jobs is extremely customer-centric. In interviews, Jobs has said the starting point for the iPod wasn't a small hard drive or a new chip, but the user experience. "Steve made some very interesting observations very early on about how this was about navigating content," Jonny Ive said about the iPod. "It was about being very focused and not trying to do too much with the device—which would have been its complication and, therefore, its demise. The enabling features aren't obvious and evident, because the key was getting rid of stuff."[4]

One of the most important parts of Apple's design process is simplification. The simplicity of Apple's products stems from choices being taken away from the customer. For Jobs, less is always more. "As technology becomes more complex, Apple's core strength of knowing how to make very sophisticated technology comprehensible to mere mortals is in even greater demand," he told the *Times*.[5]

John Sculley, Apple's CEO from 1983 to 1993, said Jobs concentrated as much on what was left out as on the stuff that was included. "What makes Steve's methodology different than everybody else's is that he always believed that the most important decisions you make are not the things that you do, but the things you decide not to do," Sculley told me.[6]

A study by Elke den Ouden of the Eindhoven University of Technology in The Netherlands found that nearly half of the products returned by consumers for refunds are in perfect working order, but their new owners couldn't figure out how to use them. She discovered that the average American consumer will fumble with a new device for only twenty minutes before giving up and returning it to the store. This was true of cell phones, DVD players, and MP3 players. More surprisingly, she asked several managers from Philips (the Dutch electronics giant is one of her clients) to take home a handful of products and use them over the weekend. The managers, most of them tech savvy, failed to get the products to work. "Product developers, brought in to witness the struggles of average consumers, were astounded by the havoc they created," she wrote.

Den Ouden concluded that the products had been poorly defined in the early design stage: no one had clearly articulated what the product's primary function was to be. As a result, designers heaped on the features and capabilities until the products became a confusing mess. This is an all too common story in consumer electronics and software design. Engineers tend to create products that only they themselves can understand. Witness early MP3 players like Creatives' Nomad Jukebox, which had an inscrutable interface that only a nerd could love.

Many consumer electronics products are designed with the notion that more features mean better value. Engineers are often pressured to add features to new versions of their products, which are marketed as "new and improved." A lot of this feature creep is driven by consumer expectations. Newer models are expected to have new capabilities; otherwise, where's the incentive to upgrade? Plus, customers tend to look for devices with the most features. More features equal better value. Apple tries to resist this. The first iPod had the hardware for FM radio and voice recording, but these features were not implemented, lest they complicate the device. "What's interesting is that out of that simplicity, an almost … unashamed sense of simplicity, and expressing it, came a very different product," Ive said. "But difference wasn't the goal. It's actually very easy to create a different thing. What was exciting is starting to realize that its difference was really a consequence of this quest to make it a very simple thing."

A lot of companies like to say they're customer-centric. They approach their users and ask them what they want. This so-called user-centric innovation is driven by feedback and focus groups. But Jobs shuns laborious studies of users locked in a conference room. He plays with the new technology himself, noting his own reactions to it, which is given as feedback to his engineers. If something is too hard to use, Jobs gives instructions for it to be simplified. Anything that is unnecessary or confusing is to be removed. If it works for him, it'll work for Apple's customers.

John Sculley told me that Jobs always focused on the user experience. "He always looked at things from the perspective of what was the users experience going to be," Sculley said. "But unlike a lot of people in product marketing in those days who would go out and do consumer testing, asking people what they wanted, Steve didn't believe in that. He said, 'How can I possibly ask someone what a graphics-based computer ought to be when they have no idea what a graphics-based computer is? No one has ever seen one before.' "[7]

Creativity in art and technology is about individual expression. Just as an artist couldn't produce a painting by conducting a focus group, Jobs doesn't use them either. Jobs can't innovate by asking a focus group what they want—they don't know what they want. Like Henry Ford once said: "If I'd asked my customers what they wanted, they'd have said a faster horse."

Patrick Whitney, director of the Illinois Institute of Technology's Institute of Design, the United States's biggest graduate school of design, said user groups aren't suited to technology innovation. Traditionally, the tech industry has conducted carefully controlled studies on new products, especially interfaces. These Human Computer Interaction studies are usually conducted after a product has been designed, to see what works as anticipated and what needs refining. By definition, these studies need users who are unfamiliar with the technology, or they will skew the study. "User groups need naïve users," Whitney explained. "But these users can't tell you what they want. You have to watch them to discover what they want."

Whitney said Sony would never have invented the Walkman if it had listened to its users. The company actually conducted a lot of research before releasing it. "All the marketing data said the Walkman was going to fail. It was unambiguous. No one would buy it. But [founder Akio] Marita pushed it through anyway. He knew. Jobs is the same. He has no need for user groups because he is a user experience expert."[8]

"We have a lot of customers, and we have a lot of research into our installed base," Jobs told *Business Week*. "We also watch industry trends pretty carefully. But in the end, for something this complicated, it's really hard to design products by focus groups. A lot of times, people don't know what they want until you show it to them."[9]

Jobs is Apple's one-man focus group. One of his great strengths is that he's not an engineer. Jobs has no formal training in engineering or programming. He doesn't have a business degree. In fact, he doesn't have a degree at all. He's a college dropout. Jobs doesn't think like an engineer. He thinks like a layman, which makes him the perfect test bed for Apple's products. He is Apple's Everyman, the ideal Apple customer. "Technically he's at the serious hobbyist level," said Dag Spicer, a senior curator with the Computer History Museum in Mountain View, California. "He had no formal training, but he's followed technology since a teenager. He's technically aware enough to follow trends, like a good stock analyst. He has a layman's view. It's a great asset."[10]

Guy Kawasaki, Apple's former chief evangelist, told me that the budget at Apple for focus groups and market research is a negative number—and he was only slightly exaggerating. Apple, like most corporations, does spend money on researching its customers, but Jobs certainly doesn't poll users when developing new products. "Steve Jobs doesn't do market research," Kawasaki said. "Market research for Steve Jobs is the right hemisphere talks to the left hemisphere."[11]

Lessons from Steve

- *Be a despot.* Someone's got to make the call. Jobs is Apple's one-man focus group. It's not how other companies do it, but it works.
- *Generate alternatives and pick the best.* Jobs insists on choices.
- *Design pixel by pixel.* Get way down in the details. Jobs paid attention to the tiniest details. You should, too.
- *Simplify.* Simplifying means stripping back. Here is Jobs's focus again: simplifying means saying "no."
- *Don't be afraid to start from scratch.* Mac OS X was worth doing over, even if it took one thousand programmers three years of nonstop toil to do it.
- *Avoid the Osborne effect.* Keep the new goodies secret until they're ready to ship, lest customers stop buying the current stuff while waiting for the new stuff.
- *Don't shit on your own doorstep.* Apple's engineers hated the old Mac OS, but Jobs ordered a positive spin on it.
- *When it comes to ideas, anything is game.* Jobs is not a design radical, but he is willing to try new things.
- *Find an easy way to present new ideas.* If it means spreading glossy sheets all over a big conference table, get a big printer.
- *Don't listen to your customers.* They don't know what they want.

Chapter 3

Perfectionism: Product Design and the Pursuit of Excellence

"Be a yardstick of quality. Some people aren't used to an environment where excellence is expected."

—Steve Jobs

I n January 1999, the day before the introduction of a new line of multicolored iMacs, Steve Jobs was practicing his product presentation at a big auditorium near Apple's HQ. A reporter from *Time* was sitting in the empty auditorium, watching as Jobs rehearsed the big moment when the new iMacs would first glide into public view. Five of the machines in a range of bright colors were mounted on a sliding pedestal hidden behind a curtain, ready to take center stage on Jobs's cue.

Jobs wanted the moment when they slid out from behind the curtain to be projected onto a large video screen looming over the stage. The technicians set it up, but Jobs didn't think the lighting was doing the translucent machines justice. The iMacs looked good onstage, but they didn't really shine on the projection screen. Jobs wanted the lights to be turned up brighter and to turn on earlier. He tells the producer to try it again. Speaking into his headset, the producer instructs the backstage crew to set it up. The iMacs slide back behind the curtain, and on cue, they slide back out again.

But the lighting is still not right. Jobs comes jogging half-way down the hall and plonks into a seat, legs dangling over the chair in front. "Let's keep doing it till we get it right, OK?" he orders.

The iMacs slide back behind the curtain and out again, but it's still not right. "No, no," he says, shaking his head. "This isn't working at all." They do it again. This time the lights are bright enough, but they're not coming on soon enough. Jobs is starting to lose patience. "I'm getting tired of asking about this," he snarls.

The crew does it a fourth time, and finally the lighting looks great. The machines sparkle on the huge projection screen. Jobs is elated. "Oh! Right there! That's great!" he shouts. "That's perfect! Wooh!"

Throughout all this, the *Time* reporter is utterly mystified why so much effort is put into a single lighting cue. It seems to be so much work for such a small part of the show. Why invest so much elbow grease in getting every single little detail just right? Earlier, Jobs had been rhapsodizing about new twist-off caps on Odwalla juice bottles, which was another puzzle to the reporter. Who cares about twist-off caps or making sure stage lights come on one second before the curtain opens? What difference do these things make?

But when the iMacs slide out, the lights beaming brightly down on them, the reporter is extremely impressed. He writes: "And you know what? He's right. The iMacs do look better when the lights come on earlier. Odwalla bottles are better with twist-off caps. The common man did want colorful computers that delivered plug-and-play access to the Internet."[1]

Jobs's Pursuit of Perfection

Jobs is a stickler for detail. He's a fussy, pain-in-the-ass perfectionist who drives subordinates crazy with his persnickety demands. But where some see picky perfectionism, others see the pursuit of excellence.

Jobs's no-compromise ethos has inspired a unique approach to developing products at Apple. Under Jobs's guidance, products are developed through nearly endless rounds of mockups and prototypes that are constantly edited and revised. This is true for both hardware and software. Products are passed back and forth among designers, programmers, engineers, and managers, and then back again. It's not serial. There are lots and lots of meetings and brainstorming sessions. The work is revised over and over, with an emphasis on simplification as it evolves. It's a fluid, iterative process that sometimes means going back to the drawing board, or scrapping the product altogether.

Like the introduction of the iMacs, things are done over and over again until they are done right. After its initial release, the iMac was continually updated. In addition to upgrading the chips and hard drives, the iMac's Bondi-blue case was replaced with a range of bright colors—at first, blueberry, grape, lime, strawberry, and tangerine; and later more sedate hues: graphite, indigo, ruby, sage, and snow.

Throughout, Jobs insists on an unprecedented attention to detail that ensures that Apple turns out products with a fit and finish worthy of an artisan. Apple's products have consistently won design awards big and small, and instill in customers a loyalty bordering on mania.

Jobs's pursuit of excellence is the secret of Apple's great design. For Jobs, design isn't decoration. It's not the surface appearance of a product. It's not about the color or the stylistic details. For Jobs, design is the way the product works. Design is *function,* not form. And to properly figure out how the product works, it has to be thoroughly hashed out in the design process. As Jobs explained in a 1996 interview with *Wired*: "Design is a funny word. Some people think design means how it looks. But of course, if you dig deeper, it's really how it works. The design of the Mac wasn't what it looked like, although that was part of it. Primarily, it was how it worked. To design something really well, you have to get it. You have to really grok what it's all about. It takes a passionate commitment to really thoroughly understand something, chew it up, not just quickly swallow it. Most people don't take the time to do that."

As the Romanian sculptor Constantin Brancusi said: "Simplicity is complexity resolved." The original Macintosh took three years to design. Three years of incredibly hard work. It wasn't knocked out in the hectic schedule typical of many technology products. It went through revision after revision. Every aspect of its design, from the precise beige of its case to the symbols on the keyboard, was exhaustively worked on, and worked on, and worked on, until it was right.

"When you start looking at a problem and think it's really simple, you don't understand how complex the problem really is," Jobs told the Mac's designers in 1983. "Once you get into the problem ... you see that it's complicated, and you come up with all these convoluted solutions. That's where most people stop, and the solutions tend to work for a while. But the really great person will keep going, find the underlying problem, and come up with an elegant solution that works on every level. That's what we wanted to do with the Mac."[2]

In the Beginning

Of course, part of design *is* aesthetics. Jobs's interest in computer aesthetics goes all the way back to the company's first computer, the Apple I. Designed by Steve Wozniak and assembled by hand in Jobs's parents' garage, the Apple I was little more than a bare-bones motherboard covered in a few chips. At the time, personal computers were sold to a tiny niche audience: bearded engineers and hobbyists. They bought their computers in parts and soldered them together on a workshop table. They added their own power supply, monitor, and case. Most built cases from wood, usually old orange crates. One put his Apple I motherboard in a leather briefcase—a lamp cord trailing out the back—to make the first laptop.

Jobs disliked this amateurish, hobbyist aesthetic. He wanted to sell finished computers to paying customers, the more the merrier. To appeal to ordinary consumers, Apple's computers had to look like real products, not half-finished Heathkits. What computers needed were nice cases that signaled their function as consumer products. The idea was to build ready-assembled computing appliances—an appliance good to go, no assembly required. Plug it in and you're ready to start computing.

Jobs's design crusade began with the Apple II, which came off the drawing board shortly after the company's incorporation in 1976. While Wozniak worked on the groundbreaking hardware (for which he won a place in the National Inventors Hall of Fame), Jobs focused on the case. "It was clear to me that for every hardware hobbyist who wanted to assemble his own computer, there were a thousand people who couldn't do that but wanted to mess around with programming... just like I did when I was 10. My dream for the Apple II was to sell the first real packaged computer... I got a bug up my rear that I wanted the computer in a plastic case."[3]

No one else was putting computers in plastic cases. To figure out what it might look like, Jobs began scouting department stores for inspiration. He found it in the kitchen section of Macy's while looking at Cuisinart food processors. Here was what the Apple II needed: a nice molded plastic case with smooth edges, muted colors, and a lightly textured surface.

Knowing nothing about industrial design, Jobs went looking for a professional designer. Typically, he started at the top. He approached two of Silicon Valley's top design firms, but was rejected because he didn't have enough money. He offered them stock in Apple, which was worthless at the time. They'd later regret that decision.

Asking around, Jobs eventually found Jerry Manock, a freelance designer who'd just left Hewlett-Packard a month before and needed work. It was a good match. Jobs only had a little money, and Manock was nearly broke. "When Steve asked me to design the case for the Apple II, it didn't occur to me to say no," he said. "But I did ask to be paid in advance."[4]

Manock designed a utilitarian case whose shape was dictated by Wozniak's motherboard. The most important consideration was that it could be quickly and cheaply cast. Manock put a sloping wedge at the front for the built-in keyboard, and made it taller at the back to accommodate the expansion slots. Jobs wanted it to look pretty when users opened the case, and asked Manock to have the cases chromed inside, but Manock ignored him and Jobs didn't press it.

To get the case ready for the Apple II's big debut at the first West Coast Computer Faire in April 1977 (which is now considered the event that heralded the birth of the personal computer industry), Manock had a small batch of cases made at a local low-price plastic molding shop. When the molds came back they were pretty rough. They had to be sanded to make the lids fit the bases, and some had to be filled and painted to look presentable. Manock prepared twenty for the Faire, but only three were finished with circuit boards inside. Jobs put these machines on the front desk. He stacked the remaining empty machines—very professionally—at the back of the booth. "Compared to the primitive stuff on view elsewhere at the Faire, our finished plastic blew everyone away," recalled Manock. "Even though Apple was only a few months old, the plastic cases made it look like we had already achieved high-volume production."[5]

The molded case helped Jobs position the Apple II as a consumer item, just as Hewlett-Packard had done with the pocket calculator. Before Bill Hewlett designed the first "pocket" calculator, most calculators were large, expensive, desktop models. Early HP marketing studies estimated that there was a market for perhaps fifty thousand pocket calculators. But Bill Hewlett instinctively felt that scientists and engineers would love a small, pocketable calculator in a slim plastic case. He was right. HP sold fifty thousand of the iconic HP-35 calculators in the first few months.

Likewise, the packaging of the Apple II in a friendly plastic case transformed the personal computer from a build-it-yourself project for geeky hobbyists into a plug-and-play appliance for ordinary consumers. Jobs had hoped the Apple II would appeal to software junkies, rather than only hobbyists interested in tinkering with electronics, and so it did. A couple of student programmers from Harvard, Dan Bricklin and Bob Frankston, created VisiCalc—the first spreadsheet—which soon became the Apple II's "killer ap." VisiCalc allowed tedious business calculations to be automated. Business ledgers that used to take hours to calculate by accountants were suddenly trivially easy to maintain. VisiCalc—and the Apple II—became a must-have for every business. Sales of the Apple II went from $770,000 in 1977 to $7.9 million in 1978—and then $49 million in 1979—making the Apple II the fastest-selling personal computer of its time.

Jobs Gets Design Religion

With the runaway success of the Apple II, Jobs started to get serious about industrial design. Design was a key differentiator between Apple's consumer-friendly, works-right-out-of-the-box philosophy and the bare-bones, utilitarian packaging of early rivals like IBM.

In March 1982, Jobs decided Apple needed a "world class"

industrial designer, a designer with an international reputation. Jerry Manock and other members of Apple's design team didn't fit the bill. In the early 1980s, design was becoming a major force in industry, especially in Europe. The success of Memphis, a product and furniture design collective from Italy, convinced Jobs that the time was right to bring the flair and quality of high design to the business of computers. Jobs was especially interested in crafting a uniform design language for all the company's products. He wanted to give the hardware the same design consistency that Apple was starting to achieve in software, and make it instantly recognizable as an Apple product. The company set up a design competition, instructing candidates plucked from design magazines like *I.D.* to draft seven products, each named after one of Snow White's dwarfs.

The winner was Hartmut Esslinger, a German industrial designer in his mid-thirties who, like Jobs, was a college dropout with strong drive and ambition. Esslinger had gained notice working for Sony designing TVs. In 1983, Esslinger emigrated to California and set up his own studio, Frog Design, Inc., providing exclusive services to Apple for an unprecedented $100,000 a month, plus billable time and expenses.[6]

For Apple, Esslinger crafted a distinct look that came to be known as the "Snow White" design language, which would dominate computer case design for a decade—and not just at Apple, but throughout the whole computer industry.

Esslinger's Snow White language was characterized by the

clever use of chamfers, bevels, and rounded corners. A good example is the Macintosh SE, an iconic all-in-one computer that's often seen these days as a fish tank. Unable to throw out their beloved machines, many owners turn them into aquariums!

Like Jobs, Esslinger had an eye for detail. One of his signature motifs was the use of vertical and horizontal stripes, which cleverly broke up the bulky lines of cases, making them seem smaller than they were.

Many of these stripes also doubled as ventilation slits, precision crafted into S-shaped cross sections, which prevented objects like paperclips being poked inside. Esslinger also insisted on using the highest quality manufacturing processes, and talked Jobs into adopting a specialized molding technique known as zero-draft. Though expensive, zero-draft molding made Apple's cases small and precise, with the kind of fit and finish Jobs approved of highly. It also made the cases very difficult for counterfeiters to copy; Apple had a problem with cheap knockoffs at the time.

Apple's Snow White designs went on to win scores of design awards, and the ideas eventually became so widely adopted by competitors that they became the unspoken industry standard for case design. All the beige computers shipped throughout the 1980s and 1990s by Dell, IBM, Compaq, and others now look pretty much the same and that's because of Snow White.

The Macintosh, Jobs's "Volkscomputer"

In 1984, while working on the original Macintosh, Jobs began to develop a design process marked by the constant revision of protoypes. Under his close guidance, Jobs charged Manock to come up with the Mac's exterior case. Then a full-time Apple employee, Manock worked closely with another talented Apple designer, Terry Oyama, who did most of the initial drafting.

Jobs wanted the Mac to be a kind of crankless Volkswagen—a cheap, democratic computer for the masses. To make his "volkscomputer" cheap to produce, Jobs took a leaf from the book of one of his heroes, Henry Ford. Jobs would offer only one configuration for the Mac, like the Model T, which notoriously was said to come in any color as long as it was black. The original Mac would come in beige, and it would have no expansion slots and very limited memory. These were controversial decisions at the time, and many predicted they would doom the machine. No one would buy such an underpowered computer that couldn't be easily upgraded. But like Ford, Jobs made the decision primarily to save money on production costs. But it also had a secondary effect that Jobs predicted would be beneficial to the consumer: it simplified the machine.

Jobs wanted the Mac to be immediately accessible to anyone who picked it up, whether they'd laid eyes on a computer before or not. He insisted the new owner shouldn't have to set it up; they shouldn't have to plug the monitor into the case; and they definitely shouldn't have to learn any arcane commands to use it.

To make it easy to set up, Jobs and the design team decided the Mac's screen, its disk drives, and its circuitry would all be housed in the same case, with a detachable keyboard and mouse that plugged in the back. This all-in-one design would allow them to dispense with all the wires and plugs of other PCs. And to make it smaller on the desk, the Mac would have a then-unusual vertical orientation. This put the disk drive below the monitor, instead of to the side like other machines at the time, which were shaped like flat pizza boxes.

The upright layout gave the Mac an anthropomorphic appearance: it looked like a face. The slot for the disk drive resembled a mouth and the keyboard recess at the bottom, the chin. Jobs seized on this. He wanted the Mac to be friendly and easy to use, and guided the design team to make the case "friendly." At first, the designers had no idea what he meant. "Even though Steve didn't draw any of the lines, his ideas and inspiration made the design what it is," Oyama said later. "To be honest, we didn't know what it meant for a computer to be 'friendly' until Steve told us."[7]

Jobs disliked the design of the Mac's predecessor, the Lisa, which had a thick band of plastic above its screen. It reminded Jobs of a Cro-Magnon forehead. He insisted the Mac's forehead be much slimmer and more intelligent. Jobs also wanted the case to be durable and scratch resistant. Manock selected a grade of tough ABS plastic—the kind used for Lego bricks—and gave it a fine texture that would disguise scuffs. Manock colored it beige, Pantone 453, which he thought would age well in sunlight. Lighter colors used in earlier machines turned an ugly bright orange. Plus, an earth tone seemed to be the best color to blend into offices and homes, and it was similar to the color Hewlett-Packard was using for its computers. And so started a trend in computers and office equipment that's lasted nearly twenty years.

Oyama made a preliminary plaster model and Jobs gathered most of the development team to critique it. Andy Hertzfeld, a key member of the team who wrote a lot of the system software, thought it was cute and attractive, and had a distinct personality. But Jobs saw room for improvement. "After everyone else had their say, Steve cut loose with a torrent of merciless criticism. 'It's way too boxy, it's got to be more curvaceous. The radius of the first chamfer needs to be bigger, and I don't like the size of the bezel. But it's a start,' " Hertzfeld wrote. "I didn't even know what a chamfer was, but Steve was evidently fluent in the language of industrial design, and extremely demanding about it."[8]

Jobs paid close attention to every detail. Even the mouse was designed to reflect the shape of the computer: it has the same dimensions, and its single square button corresponds to the shape and placement of the screen.

There was only one switch on the Mac—the on/off switch. It was put at the back, where the user couldn't accidentally hit it and turn off the computer. Because it was hidden at the back, Manock thoughtfully put a smooth area around the switch to make it easy to find by touch. By Manock's estimation, it was this kind of attention to detail that elevated the Mac into an object of historical interest. "That's the kind of detail that turns an ordinary product into an artifact," Manock said.

Jobs also gave a lot of thought to the way the Mac's design could be fashioned to determine the user's interaction with it. For example, Jobs removed all the function keys and cursor arrows, which were standard issue on keyboards at the time. Jobs didn't want users hitting function keys to interact with the machine—they would have to use the mouse instead. The absence of these keys had another, secondary effect: they forced software developers to completely rewrite their programs for the Mac interface, instead of simply porting over their Apple II software with minimal changes. The Mac's GUI represented a new way to interact with computers, and Jobs wanted to force software developers to fully embrace it.

Every month for several months, Manock and Oyama made new models, and Jobs assembled the team for their feedback. Every time there was a new model, all the old ones were lined up next to it for comparison. "By the fourth model, I could barely distinguish it from the third one, but Steve was always critical and decisive, saying he loved or hated a detail that I could barely perceive," Hertzfeld recalled. Manock and Oyama made five or six prototypes before Jobs finally gave his approval, and then they turned their attention to making it into a mass-produced case. To celebrate—and to acknowledge the artistry of the entire effort—Jobs held a "signing party," which was celebrated with champagne and the signing of the inside of the case by key members of the team. "Artists sign their work," Jobs explained.[9]

However, when the Mac was finally released in January 1984, it was seriously underpowered. To save money, Jobs had given it only 128K of memory, a fraction of what it needed. Simple operations like copying files were painful affairs requiring users to swap floppy disks in and out of the floppy disk drive. Early users loved the Mac in principle, but not in practice. "What I (and I think everybody else who bought the machine in the early days) fell in love with was not the machine itself, which was ridiculously slow and underpowered, but a romantic idea of the machine," wrote science fiction author Douglas Adams.[10]

Luckily, the Mac's primary hardware engineer, Burrell Smith, anticipated this, and secretly included the ability to expand the memory to 512K by adding several lines of extra circuitry to the Mac's main logic board—against Jobs's express orders. Thanks to Smith's thinking ahead, however, Apple was able to release a much-improved version of the Mac with more memory a few months later.

Unpacking Apple

Jobs lent his eye to *every detail* of the machine's design, including the design of the packaging. In fact, Jobs decided the first
Macintosh's packaging was going to be an integral part of
introducing consumers to his "revolutionary" computer
platform.

Back in 1984, no one outside of a few research labs had seen
anything like the Macintosh. Personal computers were used by
bespectacled engineers and hobbyists. Computers were bought
in parts and soldered together on a workshop table. They performed math calculations and were controlled by arcane commands entered at a blinking cursor.

By contrast, Jobs and the Mac team had worked up a friendly
machine with picturesque icons and menus in plain English,
all controlled by an unfamiliar pointing and clicking device—
the mouse.

To help consumers familiarize themselves with the mouse
and the Mac's other components, Jobs decided that the buyer
should have to assemble the Mac themselves out of the box.
The act of assembling the machine would introduce the user to
all its components, and give them a feel for how they worked.

All the parts—the computer, keyboard, mouse, cords, disks,
and manual—were packaged separately. Jobs helped design the
minimalist box decorated with a black-and-white picture of
the Mac and a few labels in the Apple Garamond font. At the

time, Jobs talked of "elegance" and "taste," but his packaging ideas introduced to the technology industry the "unpacking routine," a familiarization ritual that has been adopted by everyone from Dell to cell phone makers.

Apple still carefully designs its packaging with introductory lessons in mind.

In 1999, Jonathan Ive told *Fast Company* magazine that the packaging of the first iMac was carefully designed to introduce the machine to the new consumer. The iMac's accessories, keyboard, and manual were all packed in a piece of packing foam that doubled as a table to hold them. When the consumer removed this first piece of foam packaging, they saw the handle at the top of the iMac—which clearly indicated to the consumer to lift the machine out of its box and set it on a table. "That's the great thing about handles," said Ive. "You know what they're there for."[11]

The consumer then naturally turned to the accessory box, which when opened contained three cables: one for power, one for the Internet, and the other for the keyboard. Ive said the presentation of these things in that precise order—the iMac's handle, then the cables to set it up—were carefully thought out so that they clearly told the consumer, who may have never bought a computer before, the steps they needed to take to get the machine up and running. "It sounds simple and obvious," said Ive. "But often, getting to that level of simplicity requires enormous iteration in design. You have to spend considerable energy understanding the problems that exist and the issues people have—even when they find it difficult to articulate those issues and problems themselves."[12]

This kind of attention to detail can sometimes seem maniacal; and sometimes it is. Shortly before the launch of the iPod, Jobs was disappointed that the headphone jack didn't yield a satisfying click when plugging and unplugging the earphones. Dozens of sample iPods were to be given to reporters and VIPs at the product presentation. Jobs instructed an engineer to retrofit all the iPods with a new jack that would give a satisfying click.

Here's another example: At one point Jobs wanted the original Mac's motherboard redesigned for *aesthetic* reasons. Parts of the motherboard were "ugly," in his opinion, and he wanted the motherboard to be reconfigured to make for a more pleasing arrangement of chips and circuits. Naturally, his engineers were appalled. Motherboards are extremely complex pieces of technology. Their layouts are carefully designed to ensure robust and reliable connections between components. They are carefully laid out to prevent chips from coming loose, and to prevent electrical charges arcing from one circuit to another. Redesigning the motherboard to make it look pretty would not be easy. Naturally the engineers protested, saying nobody would ever see it. More important, they predicted a new arrangement wouldn't work electronically. But Jobs persisted. "A great carpenter isn't going to use lousy wood for the back of a cabinet, even though nobody's going to see it," Jobs said.

Grudgingly, the hardware engineers created a new design, investing several thousand dollars to produce a prettier circuit board. But, as predicted, the new motherboard didn't work, and Jobs was forced to drop the idea.[13]

Jobs's insistence on excellence sometimes delays products; and he's quite willing to kill projects that his team has worked on for years. But his unwillingness to compromise ensures that Apple products are never rushed out of the door until they are polished to his satisfaction.

The Great Washing Machine Debate

Jobs famously lived in a mansion in the early eighties that was nearly empty of furniture because he couldn't bear substandard furnishings. He slept on a mattress, surrounded by a few giant photographic prints. Eventually he bought a German grand piano, even though he didn't play, because he admired its design and craftsmanship. When Apple's former CEO John Sculley visited Jobs, he was shocked by the unkempt appearance of the house. It looked abandoned, especially compared to the perfectly manicured palaces surrounding it. "I'm sorry I don't have much furniture," Jobs apologized to Sculley, "I just haven't gotten around to it."[14]

Sculley said Jobs was unwilling to settle for anything but the best. "I remember going to Steve's house and he had no furniture, he just had a picture of Einstein, whom he admired greatly, and he had a Tiffany lamp and a chair and a bed." Sculley told me. "He just didn't believe in having lots of things around, but he was incredibly careful what he selected."[15]

Jobs has a lot of trouble shopping. He can't decide on a cell phone. "I end up not buying a lot of things," he said in response to a query about what gadgets and technologies he buys, "because I find them ridiculous."[16]

When he does go shopping, the process can be laborious. Searching for a new washing machine and dryer, Jobs roped his whole family into a two-week debate about which model to select. The Jobs family didn't base its decision on a quick glance at the features and the price, like most other families would. Instead, the discussion revolved around American versus European design, the amount of water and detergent consumed, the speed of the wash, and the longevity of the clothes.

"We spent some time in our family talking about what's the trade-off we want to make. We ended up talking a lot about design, but also about the values of our family. Did we care most about getting our wash done in an hour versus an hour and a half? Or did we care most about our clothes feeling really soft and lasting longer? Did we care about using a quarter of the water? We spent about two weeks talking about this every night at the dinner table. We'd get around to that old washer-dryer discussion. And the talk was about design."[17]

In the end, Jobs opted for German appliances, which he thought were "too expensive" but washed clothes well with little water and detergent. "They are really wonderfully made and one of the few products we've bought over the last few years that we're all really happy about," Jobs said. "These guys really thought the process through. They did such a great job designing these washers and dryers. I got more thrill out of them than I have out of any piece of high tech in years."

The great washing machine debate seems excessive, but Jobs brings the same values—and the same process—to the task of developing products at Apple. Industrial design at Apple isn't treated as the final gloss on a product that's already been engineered, as it is at many other companies. Too many companies treat design as the skin slapped on at the last minute. In fact, at many companies, design is outsourced altogether. A separate firm will handle how the product looks— just as a separate firm will likely handle manufacturing.

"It's sad and frustrating that we are surrounded by products that seem to testify to a complete lack of care," said Ive, the affable Brit who heads up Apple's small design team. "That's an interesting thing about an object. One object speaks volumes about the company that produced it and its values and priorities."

Apple outsources most of its manufacturing, but not the design of its products. Quite the opposite. Apple's industrial designers are intimately involved from the very first meeting.

Jonathan Ive, the Designer

An Englishman in his late thirties, Ive has a muscular wrestler's build and his hair is closely cropped. But Jonathan Ive is friendly and approachable. He is extremely soft-spoken, almost shy, which is quite unusual for someone in his position at the top of a hard-driving corporation like Apple. He's so retiring, he once had Jobs get up on stage to accept an award for him, even though he was sitting right there in the audience.

He won a major design award twice while still a student, the only undergraduate to have ever done so. Since then the awards have come thick and fast. Thanks to a string of highly influential products, from the iMac to the iPhone, Ive has twice been named Designer of the Year by London's prestigious Design Museum. In 2006, he was made a Commander of the British Empire, an honor awarded by the British monarch.

Ive can be hard to pin down on specifics. He has a tendency to talk in the abstract, and sometimes slips into corporate speak. He deflects personal questions, but get him talking about design and it's hard to shut him up. He talks design with great enthusiasm, gesticulating passionately and scrunching his fingers for emphasis.

At one of Apple's product presentations, I asked him for a couple of quick comments about the design of the aluminum case that houses Apple's high-end professional workstations (the same case has been used for several years in a string of products, from the Power Mac G5 in 2003 to the current Mac Pro), which are made from austere slabs of raw aluminum that are as unadorned as the alien monolith in the movie *2001, A Space Odyssey*.

He was only too delighted to describe the philosophy—and all the hard work—behind the design of the machine. "I guess every time you do something, you feel particularly pleased with something you just developed," he said. "This one was really hard." Ive walked over to a display model sitting nearby. He indicated its plain aluminum case. "There's an applied style of being minimal and simple, and then there's real simplicity," he said. "This looks simple, because it really is."

Ive said keeping it simple was the overall design philosophy for the machine. "We wanted to get rid of anything other than what was absolutely essential, but you don't see that effort," he said. "We kept going back to the beginning again and again. 'Do we need that part? Can we get it to perform the function of the other four parts?' It became an exercise to reduce and reduce, but it makes it easier to build and easier for people to work with."

Ive then launched into a passionate twenty-minute tour and description of the new computer's design. He would have gone on longer if he hadn't been cut short by a member of Apple's PR team, who reminded him he had other appointments. Ive couldn't help himself. Design is his vocation. Get him started, and he'll talk at length with great sincerity and enthusiasm about the design of something as deceptively simple as a latch for an access panel. In parting, I asked Ive to compare the Power Mac G5 to high-design computers from the world of Windows PCs, such as those from Alienware or Falcon Northwest. These machines have sometimes tended to look like hot rod muscle cars, decorated with painted flames or chrome grills.

"It's really much more potent when you don't put on a veneer pretending to be powerful," he said. "I see it as a tool. It's an extremely powerful tool. There's not a plastic façade that adds to the fact that it's a really powerful tool. It's very, very obvious that it is what it is." He continued, "From a designer's point of view, it's not an appearance game we're playing. It is very utilitarian. It's the use of material in a very minimalist way."

Ive's impromptu tour of the aluminum computer case reveals a lot about the design process that produced it: the drive to reduce and simplify, the attention to detail, and a respect for materials. Plus there's Ive's passion and drive. All of these factors contribute to Ive's unique design process.

A Penchant for Prototyping

Jonathan Ive and his wife, Heather, live with their young twins in a house near the top of Twin Peaks overlooking San Francisco. The house is described as "unostentatious," but Ive drives a James Bond car—a $200,000 Aston Martin.

Ive originally wanted to design cars. He took a course at London's Central Saint Martins Art School but found the other students too weird. "They were making 'vroom, vroom' noises as they did their drawings," he said.[18] He enrolled in a product design course at Newcastle Polytechnic instead.

It was at Newcastle that Ive developed a penchant for prototyping. Clive Grinyer, a fellow student and later one of Ive's colleagues, remembers visiting Ive's Newcastle apartment. He was flabbergasted to find it filled with hundreds of foamcore models of his final-year project: a hearing aid and microphone combination to help teachers communicate with deaf pupils. Most of the other design students built five or six models of their projects. Ive was "more focused than anyone I'd ever met on what he was trying to achieve," Grinyer said.[19]

Oddly, Ive had no affinity for computers as a student. "I went through college having a real problem with computers," Ive said. "I was convinced that I was technically inept."[20] But just before leaving Newcastle in 1989, he discovered the Mac. "I remember being astounded at just how much better it was than anything else I had tried to use," he said. "I was struck by the care taken with the whole user experience. I had a sense of connection via the object with the designers. I started to learn more about the company: how it had been founded, its values and its structure. The more I learnt about this cheeky—almost rebellious—company, the more it appealed to me, as it unapologetically pointed to an alternative in a complacent and creatively bankrupt industry. Apple stood for something and had a reason for being that wasn't just about making money."

Over the years, computers have grown on him. In an interview with *Face* magazine, he explained that he's fascinated by their multifunction nature. "There's no other product that changes function like the computer," he said. "The iMac can be a jukebox, a tool for editing video, a way to organize photographs. You can design on it, write on it. Because what it does is so new, so changeable, it allows us to use new materials, to create new forms. The possibilities are endless. I love that."

After leaving Newcastle, Ive cofounded the Tangerine design collective in London in 1989, where he worked on a wide range of products, from toilets to hair combs. But he found contract work frustrating. As an outsider, he had little influence on the outcome of his ideas within the company.

In 1992, he got a call from Apple asking him to submit some concepts for early laptops. Apple was so impressed, Ive was hired as a designer and moved to California. But as Apple went into decline during this period, design was relegated to a dusty basement. Apple's managers started to look to the competition for inspiration. They wanted focus groups. Ive came close to quitting. He worked independently and alone. He'd continue to design prototype products, but they often never got any further than a shelf in his office.

Of course, things have been very different since Jobs returned. Ive is the same designer he used to be, but the outcomes are the polar opposite.

Ive heads up a relatively small team of about a dozen industrial designers, who have worked together at Apple for many years. "We have assembled a heavenly design team," Ive says.[21] The team works in a very private studio set apart from the rest of Apple's campus. Housed in a nondescript building, the studio is sealed off from most of Apple employees for fear of re-vealing upcoming goodies. Access is granted only to a select few with authorized electronic passes; doors and windows are shaded behind black privacy glass. Even former CEO John Sculley was locked out of the design studio. "Talk about a pissed-off executive," said Robert Brunner, the head of the de-sign group at the time.[22]

There's very little personal space inside the studio. There are no cubicles or offices. The studio is a large open space with sev-eral communal design areas. It is full of expensive, state-of-the-art prototyping machines: 3D printers, powerful CAD (Computer Aided Design) workstations, and CNC (Computer Numerical Control) machine tools. There's also a massive sound system pumping out electronica all day, some of it sent from Ive's friends back home in Britain. Ive is a confessed mu-sic nut, and a close friend of top techno DJ John Digweed.

When it comes to tools, no expense is spared. But instead of hiring more and more designers, Ive puts his resources into prototyping machinery. "By keeping the core team small and investing significantly in tools and process we can work with a level of collaboration that seems particularly rare," Ive said. "In fact, the memory of how we work will endure beyond the prod-ucts of our work."[23]

The small, intimate team is key to being creative and pro-ductive, Ive says. He denies that Apple's innovations came from one individual designer or another, but the team working together. It's a process of "collectively learning stuff and getting better at what we do. One of the hallmarks of the team is inquisitiveness, being excited about being wrong because that means you've discovered something new."[24]

Whenever he talks about his work, Ive always emphasizes the team. He has no ego. After Digweed first met Ive, it took him months to discover what Ive's real role was at Apple. "Jonathan was saying how they'd designed different things and I'm sitting there thinking, 'Oh, my God. His work is used by creative people across the world every day but he has no ego about it.' "[25]

Ive's Design Process

Ive has often said that the simplicity of Apple's designs is deceiving. To a lot of people, the products seem obvious. They are so plain and simple, there seems to be no "design" involved at all. There are no frills or accoutrements that trumpet the design process. But to Ive, that's the point. The task, Ive said, is "to solve incredibly complex problems and make their resolution appear inevitable and incredibly simple, so you have no sense how difficult this thing was."[26]

The simplicity is the outcome of a design process characterized by generating a lot of ideas and then refining them—the same way the interface for OS X was designed. The process involves multiple teams at Apple, not just the designers. Engineers, programmers, and even marketers are also involved. Ive's

industrial designers are involved from the get-go of every project. "We get involved really early on," said Ive. "There's a very
natural, consistent collaboration with Steve, with the hardware
and software people. I think that's one of the things that's distinctive at Apple. When we're developing ideas there's not a final architecture established. I think it's in those early stages
when you're still very open to exploration, that you find opportunities."[27]

To find these opportunities, Jobs assiduously avoids a serial, step-by-step design regime, where products are passed
from one team to the next, and there's little back and forth between the different departments. This is not always the case at
other companies. Jobs has said it's like seeing a cool prototype
car at a car show, but when the production model appears four
years later, it sucks. "And you go, What happened? They had it!
They had it in the palm of their hands! They grabbed defeat
from the jaws of victory! . . . What happened was, the designers
came up with this really great idea. Then they take it to the engineers, and the engineers go, 'Nah, we can't do that. That's impossible.' And so it gets a lot worse. Then they take it to the
manufacturing people, and they go, 'We can't build that!' And
it gets a lot worse."[28]

In interviews, Ive has talked about "deep collaboration,"
"cross pollination," and "concurrent engineering." Products
being developed at Apple aren't passed from team to team,
from the designers to the engineers to the programmers, and
finally to the marketers. The design process isn't sequential.

Instead, the products are worked on by all these groups simultaneously, and there's round after round of reviews.

The meetings are endless. They're an integral part of the "deep collaborative" process, and without them there wouldn't be the same amount of "cross pollination." "The historical way of developing products just doesn't work when you're as ambitious as we are," Ive told *Time*. "When the challenges are that complex, you have to develop a product in a more collaborative, integrated way."

The design process begins with a lot of sketching. Ive's team works together, critiquing each other's ideas and incorporating feedback from the engineers and, of course, Jobs himself. The team then works up 3D computer models in various CAD applications, which are used to make physical models in foamcore and other prototyping materials. The team will often build several models, testing not only the outside shape of the new product, but the interior as well. Prototypes precisely modeling interior space and the thickness of the walls are sent to hardware engineers, who check that the internal components fit. They also make sure there's sufficient airflow through the case, and that interior components like ports and battery compartments line up.

"We make a lot of models and prototypes, and we go back and iterate," Ive said. "We strongly believe in prototyping and making things so you can pick them up and touch them." The number of models made is exhausting. "We make lots and lots

of prototypes: the number of solutions we make to get one solution is quite embarrassing, but it's a healthy part of what we
do," Ive said.[29]

Robert Brunner, a partner at Pentagram Design and former
head of Apple's Design Group, said, crucially, Apple's prototypes are always designed with the manufacturing process very
much in mind. "Apple's designers spend 10 percent of their
time doing traditional industrial design: coming up with ideas,
drawing, making models, brainstorming," he said. "They spend
90 percent of their time working with manufacturing, figuring
out how to implement their ideas."

The method is akin to a technique known to psychologists
studying problem solving as "generate and test." To solve a
problem, all the possible solutions are generated and then
tested to see if they offer a solution. It's a form of trial and error, but not as random; it's more guided and purposeful.
Apple's designers create dozens of possible solutions, constantly testing their work to see if it is approaching a solution.
The process is essentially the same as techniques used in a lot
of creative endeavors, from writing to creating music. A writer
will often start by banging out a rough draft, spilling out words
and ideas with little thought for structure or cohesion, and
then go back and edit their work, sometimes multiple times.
"Trying to simplify and refine is enormously challenging,"
Ive said.[30]

Attention to Detail: Invisible Design

Ive's team pays attention to the kind of details that other companies often overlook, like simple on/off lights and power adapters. The power cord of the first iMac was translucent—like the computer it plugged into—revealing the three twisted wires inside. Few other manufacturers pay such close attention to seemingly insignificant details. But doing so distinguishes Apple from other companies. This kind of attention to the little things is usually reserved to handcrafted goods. Apple products have those little touches that are more characteristic of bespoke suits or handmade pottery than mass-produced items churned out of Asian factories. "I think one thing that is typical about our work at Apple is caring about the smallest details," Ive said. "I think sometimes that's seen as more of a craft activity than a mass-production one. But I think that's very important."[31]

Even the insides of the machines are carefully pored over. At an exhibit at the Design Museum, Ive displayed a dismantled laptop so that visitors could see the careful design of its interior layout. "You can see our preoccupation with a part of the product that you'll never see," Ive said.[32]

Many of Apple's products are characterized by this kind of invisible design. Recent-model iMacs are large, flat screens with the computer housed behind. The screen is attached to a pedestal made from a single piece of aluminum bent at an angle to form a foot. The aluminum pedestal allows the screen to tilt back and forth with a gentle push. But getting it to move so effortlessly, and to stay in place, was the result of months of work. The computer had to be perfectly balanced to ensure the screen stayed in place. "This was very difficult to get right," Ive said at a design conference.

The foot of the iMac's aluminum base is made from a special nonslip material to prevent the machine from shifting when the screen is tilted. Why a special material? Because Ive doesn't like rubber feet. Rubber feet would have been trivially easy to add to the base, and few people would notice whether they were there or not. But to Ive, using rubber feet doesn't advance the state of the art.

Ive also hates stickers. A lot of Apple products have product information laser etched right into the case, even their unique serial numbers. It's obviously a lot simpler to slap a sticker on a product, but laser etching is another way that Apple has advanced the way products are made.

Materials and Manufacturing Processes

There have been several distinct stages in the design of Apple's products over the last few years, from fruity-colored iMacs to black MacBook laptops. Every four years or so, Apple's design "language" changes. In the late 1990s, Apple's products were distinguished by the use of brightly colored translucent plastic (the eBook and first Bondi-blue iMac). Then, in the early 2000s, Apple started making products from white polycarbonate plastic and shiny chrome (the iPod, the iBook, the Luxo-lamp iMac). Then came laptops in metals like titanium and aluminum (the PowerBook and MacBook Pro). More recently, Apple has started to use black plastic, brushed aluminum, and glass (the iPhone, iPod nano, the Intel-powered iMacs, and MacBook laptops).

The transitions between Apple's different design phases are not planned ahead of time, at least not consciously. Rather, the transition between design phases is gradual—first one product sports a new design, then another. And it follows naturally from experimentation with new materials and production methods. As Apple's designers learn how to work with a new material, they start to use it in more and more products. Take aluminum, a difficult metal to work with, which made its first appearance in the PowerBook's casing in January 2003. Then the metal was used for the Power Mac's case in June 2003, and the iPod mini in January 2004. Aluminum is now used in a lot of Apple's products, from the back of the iPhone to the iMac's keyboard.

Ive has said many times that Apple's design is never forced. The designers never say to each other, "Let's make an organic, feminine-looking computer." The iMac may look friendly and approachable, but that was never part of the machine's design brief. Instead, Apple's designers say, "Let's see what we can do with plastics, maybe we can make a translucent computer." And it proceeds from there.

Ive and his designers pay close attention to materials and material science. For many companies, materials are an afterthought in the production process. But for Ive and his design team, the materials come first. The first iMac, for example, was always intended to be "an unashamedly plastic product," Ive has explained. But plastic is usually associated with cheap. To make the iMac classy instead of chintzy, the team decided to make the computer's shell transparent. But initially they encountered problems with spotting and streaking—the clear plastic cases weren't coming off the production line uniformly clear. To ensure color consistency, the design team visited a candy factory, where they learned about mass-production tinting processes.

Talking about the aluminum foot of the recent-model, flat-panel iMac, Ive said, "I love that we took one raw piece of material—a thick piece of aluminum—and achieved that sort of utility: you bend it, stamp a hole into it and anodize it.... We spent time in Northern Japan talking to a master of metal-forming, to get a certain kind of detail. We love taking things to pieces, understanding how things are made. The product architecture starts to be informed by really understanding the material."[33]

As well as materials, Ive and his team are keen students of new manufacturing processes. The team is constantly on the lookout for new ways of making things, and some of Apple's most iconic designs are products of new manufacturing techniques. Several generations of the iPod, for example, had a thin transparent fascia bonded to the top of its plastic body. This thin coating of transparent plastic gave the iPod the appearance of extra heft and depth, without adding extra heft or depth. It also gave it a much more sophisticated look than a simple flat plastic surface.

The thin sheet of transparent plastic is the product of a plastic molding technique known as "twin-shot," where two different kinds of plastic are injected into a mold simultaneously and bond together seamlessly. As a result, the iPod's front appears to be made from two different materials—but there are no visible seams connecting them.

"We can now do things with plastic that we were previously told were impossible," Ive told the Design Museum. "Twin shooting materials gives us a range of functional and formal opportunities that really didn't exist before. The iPod is made from twin-shot plastic with no fasteners and no battery doors, enabling us to create a design which was dense and completely sealed." [34]

Before the iPod, Ive's team had been experimenting with these new molding techniques in a series of products made from clear plastic, including the Cube, several flat-panel studio monitors, and a speaker and subwoofer set for Harman Kardon. The iPod appeared fresh and new, but its look was actually the result of several years of experimentation with new molding techniques. "Some of the white products we've done are just an extension of that," says Ive.

The ability to make seamless objects led to a design decision on the iPod that's been bitterly criticized by consumers—the inability to change the iPod's battery. The iPod's battery is tightly sealed inside the device's body, inaccessible to most owners unless they are willing to prise off the metal back. Apple and several third-party companies offer battery replacement services, but at extra charge.

Apple has said the battery is designed to last for many years, often longer than the useful life of the iPod, but to some consumers the sealed battery smacks of planned obsolescence, or worse—it makes the iPod seem disposable.

Lessons from Steve

- *Don't compromise.* Jobs's obsession with excellence has created a unique development process that churns out truly great products.
- *Design is* function, *not form.* For Jobs, design is the way the product *works.*
- *Hash it out.* Jobs thoroughly figures out how the product works during the design process.
- *Include everyone.* Design isn't just for designers. Engineers, programmers, and marketers can help figure out how a product works.
- *Avoid a serial process.* Jobs constantly passes prototype products between teams, not one team to the next.
- *Generate and test.* Use trial and error—creating and editing—to make an "embarrassing" number of solutions to get to one solution.
- *Don't force it.* Jobs doesn't try to conciously design a "friendly" product. The "friendliness" emerges from the design process.
- *Respect materials.* The iMac was plastic. The iPhone is glass. Their forms follow the materials they are made from.

Chapter 4

Elitism: Hire Only *A* Players, Fire the Bozos

"In our business, one person can't do anything anymore. You create a team of people around you."

—Steve Jobs, Smithsonian Institution Oral and Video Histories

Steve Jobs has a reputation as the boss from hell, a terror-inspiring taskmaster who's forever screaming at workers and randomly firing hapless underlings. But throughout his career, Jobs has struck up a long string of productive partnerships—both personal and corporate. Jobs's success has greatly depended on attracting great people to do great work for him. He's always chosen great collaborators—from his Apple cofounder Steve Wozniak to the London-born design genius Jonathan Ive, who's responsible for the iMac, iPod, and other iconic designs.

Jobs has successfully struck up working relationships with some of the most creative people in his field, relationships that frequently last for many years. He's also forged (mostly) harmonious relationships with some of the world's top brands—Disney, Pepsi, and the big record labels. Not only does he choose great creative partners, he also brings out the best in them. Through judicious use of both the carrot and the stick, Jobs has managed to retain and motivate lots of top-shelf talent.

Jobs is an elitist who believes that a small A team is far more effective than armies of engineers and designers. Jobs has always sought out the highest quality in people, products, and advertising. Unlike a lot of companies that recruit more and more staff as they get bigger, Jobs has kept the core of Apple relatively small, especially the key A team of select designers, programmers, and executives. Many of Jobs's A team have worked at Apple, and for Jobs, for years. After he returned to Apple, most of the company's top management were executives he brought with him from NeXT. It's not easy working for Jobs, but those who can weather it tend to be loyal.

Jobs's strategy is to hire the smartest programmers, engineers, and designers available. He works hard to maintain their allegiance with stock options, and fosters the identity of small working groups. "I always considered part of my job was to keep the quality level of people in the organizations I work with very high," said Jobs. "That's what I consider one of the few things I actually can contribute individually to—to really try to instill in the organization the goal of only having 'A' players. In everything I've done it really pays to go after the best people in the world."[1]

In Jobs's view, there's not much difference between a bad taxi driver and a good one, or a bad restaurant cook and a good one. Jobs has said that a good taxi driver is maybe two or three times as good as a bad one. In the taxi-driving profession, there aren't that many levels of skill dividing good from bad. But when it comes to industrial design or programming, the difference between good and bad is vast. A good designer is one hundred or two hundred times better than a poor one. In programming, there are many, many levels of skill separating great programmers from mediocre ones, Jobs believes.[2]

Jobs is the kind of person who wants the best—the best car, the best private jet, the best pen, and the best employees. "He does tend to polarize things," Jim Oliver, Jobs's former personal assistant, told me. "People are geniuses, or bozos. There was a Pilot pen that was his favorite. All the others are 'crap.'" When working on the Mac, everyone not on the Mac team—even inside Apple—were "bozos." "There was a lot of elitism at the company," said Daniel Kottke, a close friend of Jobs's who traveled with him around India. "Steve definitely cultivated this idea that everyone else in the industry were bozos."[3]

Jobs's first partner, and perhaps the most important, was his high school friend Steve Wozniak. Wozniak was the nerdy hardware genius who made his own PC because he couldn't afford to buy one. It was Jobs who thought of making and selling

Wozniak's designs, and arranged for them to be assembled by their teenage friends in a garage. He also arranged for them to be sold at a local hobbyist electronics store. Jobs was soon recruiting outside talent to grow the company and develop its products. True to form, Jobs tried to persuade the two top design firms in Silicon Valley to design Apple's early computers, but couldn't afford them. Since then, Jobs has followed the same modus operandi—recruit and retain the best, from the original Mac team to the storytellers at Pixar.

Pixar: Art Is a Team Sport

Jobs's dedication to building an A team is best illustrated by Pixar, the animation studio he sold to Disney in 2006 for $7.4 billion. In 1995, Pixar released *Toy Story*, the first feature-length, computer-animated movie, which went on to become the highest grossing film of the year and won an Oscar. Every year since 1995, Pixar has released one hit after another—*A Bug's Life*, *Toy Story 2*, *Monsters Inc.*, *Finding Nemo*. The movies have earned $3.3 billion and won a clutch of Oscars and Golden Globes. It's a remarkable record, unrivaled by any other studio in Hollywood. Even more remarkable, it was achieved by flipping Hollywood's traditional working method on its head.

Pixar is headquartered in several smoked-glass-and-steel buildings on a leafy campus in Emeryville, a former port town across the bay from San Francisco. The campus has a relaxed, collegial atmosphere. It boasts all the perks of a high-tech,

twenty-first-century workplace: swimming pools, movie the-
aters, and a cafeteria with a wood-burning stove. Everywhere
there is whimsy: full-size statues of animated characters, door-
ways disguised as swinging bookshelves, a reception desk that
sells toys. Instead of cubicles, the company's animators work
in their own private huts, literally garden huts assembled in a
row, like a string of beach huts, each idiosyncratically decorated—a tiki hut, for example, could be next to a mini medieval
castle with a mock moat.

Pixar is run by Ed Catmull, a friendly, soft-spoken pioneer
of CGI, or computer-generated imagery, who invented some of
the key technologies that make computer animation possible.
Since the acquisition of Pixar by Disney in January 2006, Catmull has become president of the combined Pixar and Disney
Animation Studios. The storytelling heart of the company is
John Lasseter, Pixar's Academy Award–winning creative genius. A big, avuncular man who normally dresses in colorful
Hawaiian shirts, Lasseter has directed four Pixar blockbusters:
Toy Story 1 and *2*, *A Bug's Life*, and *Cars*. Lasseter is now the chief
creative officer at Disney, where he's charged with spreading
some of Pixar's magic around the tarnished Disney animation
division.

At Apple, Jobs is a hands-on micromanager. But at Pixar,
Jobs pretty much stays away, leaving the day-to-day running in
the capable hands of Catmull and Lasseter. For years, he was
pretty much a benevolent benefactor who cut checks and negotiated deals. "If I knew in 1986 how much it was going to cost

to keep Pixar going, I doubt if I would have bought the company," Jobs complained to *Fortune* in September 1995.

"I refer to those guys as the Father, the Son, and the Holy Ghost," jokes Brad Bird, director of Pixar's *The Incredibles*. "Ed, who invented this cool medium and is the designer of the human machine that is Pixar, is the Father. John, its driving creating force, is the Son. And you-know-who is the Holy Ghost."[4]

According to authors Polly LaBarre and William C. Taylor, who profiled Pixar for their book *Mavericks at Work*, the culture of Pixar is the opposite of Hollywood, which is based on hiring moviemakers *under contract*. In Tinseltown, studios hire the talent they need to make a movie on a freelance basis. The producer, the director, the actors, and the crew all work under contract. Everyone is a free agent, and as soon as the movie is wrapped, they move on. "The problem with the Hollywood model is that it's generally the day you wrap production that you realize you've finally figured out how to work together," Randy S. Nelson, the dean of Pixar University,[5] told Taylor and LaBarre.

Pixar functions on the opposite model. At Pixar, the directors, scriptwriters, and crew are all salaried employees with big stock option grants. Pixar's movies may have different directors, but the same core team of writers, directors, and animators work on them all as company employees.

In Hollywood, studios fund story ideas—the famous Hollywood pitch, the big concept. Instead of funding pitches and story ideas, Pixar funds the career development of its employees. As Nelson explains: "We've made the leap from an idea-centered business to a people-centered business. Instead of developing ideas, we develop people. Instead of investing in ideas, we invest in people."

At the heart of the company's "people investment" culture is Pixar University, an on-the-job training program that offers hundreds of courses in art, animation, and filmmaking. All of Pixar's employees are encouraged to take classes in whatever they like, whether it's relevant to their job or not. At other studios, there's a clear distinction between the "creatives," the "techies," and the crew. But Pixar's unique culture doesn't distinguish between them—everyone who works on the movies is considered an artist. Everyone works together to tell stories, and as such, everyone is encouraged to devote at least four hours of the workweek to class. The classes are filled with people from all levels of the organization: janitors sit next to department heads. "We're trying to create a culture of learning, filled with lifelong learners," said Nelson.[6]

At Pixar, they say "art is a team sport." It's a mantra, oft repeated. No one can make a movie alone, and a team of good storytellers can fix a bad story, but a poor team cannot. If a script isn't working, the whole team works together to fix it. The writers, the animators, and the director all pitch in without regard to their official role or job title. "This model tackles one of the most enduring people problems in any industry: How do you not only attract wildly talented people to work in your company, but also get those wildly talented people to continuously produce great work together?" said LaBarre.

The answer is that Pixar has created a nurturing, fun place to work. In Hollywood, filmmakers spend a lot of time jockeying for advantage, stabbing collaborators in the back to gain advantage, and constantly worrying whether they are in or out. It's hypercompetitive, insecure, and burns people out. At Pixar, the process is all about collaboration, teamwork, and learning. There's pressure, of course, especially when movies approach deadlines, but the workplace is generally nurturing and supportive. The opportunity to learn, to create, and, most of all, to work with other talented people is the reward. Plus the generous stock options, of course. At Pixar, the animators are getting rich and having fun, too. As the Latin inscription on the Pixar University crest says *Alienus Non Diutius*, Alone No Longer.

As a result, Pixar has poached some of the best animation talent in Hollywood. Other top Pixar animators include Andrew Stanton (*Finding Nemo*), Brad Bird (*The Incredibles*, *Ratatouille*), and Pete Docter (*Monsters Inc.*) who have all been aggressively headhunted by competitors. For many years Lasseter had a standing offer from Disney to jump ship, which he resisted because of the unique creative work environment at Pixar. None of the other studios could compete, not even Disney. As Jobs boasted: "Pixar's got by far and away the best computer graphics talent in the entire world, and it now has the best animation and artistic talent in the whole world to do these kinds of film. There's really no one else in the world who could do this stuff. It's really phenomenal. We're probably close to ten years ahead of anybody else."[7]

The Original Mac Team

At Apple, Jobs takes a similar view: the talent on staff is a competitive advantage that puts the company ahead of its rivals. Jobs tries to find the best people in a given field and put them on the payroll. When Jobs was conducting his product review after returning to the company, he "steved" most of Apple's products, but he made sure to keep the best talent on staff, among them designer Jonathan Ive. When Jobs wanted to open a chain of Apple retail stores in 2001, the first thing he did, *the very first thing*, was find the best person in retail to advise him. Jobs was afraid of getting burned, and so went looking for an expert. "We looked at it and said, 'You know, this is probably really hard, and really easy for us to get our head handed to us,'" Jobs told *Fortune* magazine. "So we did a few things. No. 1, I started asking who was the best retail executive at the time. Everybody said [Millard] Mickey Drexler, who was running the Gap." Jobs recruited Drexler to sit on Apple's board and advise the company as it got Apple's retail chain off the ground (more on the stores later).

Jobs's first A team—Bill Atkinson, Andy Hertzfeld, Burrell Smith, et al.—was assembled in 1980 to build the original Mac and they worked under a pirate flag at Apple HQ.

The core of the Mac team was assembled by Jef Raskin, the original Mac team leader, but Jobs did a lot of the recruiting himself. He pulled in talent from all over Apple and Silicon Valley, without regard to job title or experience. If he judged someone fit to contribute, he did everything he could to recruit them. Bruce Horn, for example, a programmer who created the Mac's Finder—the heart of the Mac's operating system—didn't initially want to work at Apple, until he was seduced by Jobs. Horn had just taken a job with another company, VTI, which promised him a $15,000 signing bonus, a large sum of money at the time. Then Jobs called.

Horn recalled:

> On Friday evening, I got a phone call. "Bruce, it's Steve. What do you think about Apple?" It was Steve Jobs. "Well, Steve, Apple's cool, but I accepted a job at VTI."
>
> "You did what? Forget that, you get down here tomorrow morning, we have a lot more things to show you. Be at Apple at 9 a.m." Steve was adamant. I thought I'd go down, go through the motions, and then tell him that I'd made up my mind and was going to VTI.
>
> Steve switched on the Reality Distortion Field full-force. I met with seemingly everyone on the Mac team, from Andy to Rod Holt to Jerry Manock to the other soft-

ware engineers, and back to Steve. Two full days of demos, drawings of the various designs, marketing presentations—I was overwhelmed.

On Monday I called Doug Fairbairn at VTI and told him I had changed my mind.[8]

Once he'd assembled his team, Jobs gave them the freedom to be creative and shielded them from the growing bureaucracy at Apple, which tried several times to shut down the Mac project because they viewed it as an unimportant distraction. "The people who are doing the work are the moving force behind the Macintosh. My job is to create a space for them, to clear out the rest of the organization and keep it at bay,"[9] Jobs wrote in a 1984 essay that was printed in the inaugural issue of *Macworld* magazine. Hertzfeld put it more bluntly: "The most important thing Steve did was erect a giant shit-deflecting umbrella that protected the project from the evil suits across the street."[10]

As well as recruiting the best talent, Jobs is quick to get rid of those who don't measure up. Hiring only insanely great employees and firing the bozos has been one of Jobs's longest held managerial principles. "It's painful when you have some people who are not the best people in the world and you have to get rid of them; but I found that my job has sometimes exactly been that—to get rid of some people who didn't measure up and I've always tried to do it in a humane way. But nonetheless it has to be done and it is never fun," Jobs said in a 1995 interview.[11]

Small Is Beautiful

Jobs likes to work in small teams. He didn't want the original Mac team to exceed one hundred members, lest it became unfocused and unmanageable. Jobs firmly believes that small teams of talented employees run circles around larger groups. At Pixar, Jobs tried to ensure that the company never grew to more than a few hundred people. When asked to compare Apple and Pixar, Jobs attributed much of its success to its small size. "Apple has some pretty amazing people, but the collection of people at Pixar is the highest concentration of remarkable people that I have ever witnessed," Jobs told *Fortune* in 1998. "There's a person who's got a Ph.D. in computer-generated plants—3-D grass and trees and flowers. There's another who is the best in the world at putting imagery on film. Also, Pixar is more multidisciplinary than Apple ever will be. But the key thing is that it is much smaller. Pixar's got 450 people. You could never have the collection of people that Pixar has now if you went to two thousand people."

Jobs's philosophy harks back to the old days when he, Wozniak, and a few teenage friends assembled computers by hand in a garage. To some extent, Jobs's preference for small development teams at Apple today is the same thing: a simulation of a garage startup inside a big company with more than 21,000 employees.

On returning to Apple in 1997, Jobs set about assembling an A team to resurrect the company. Several of the top executives he appointed had worked with him before at NeXT, including Jon Rubinstein, who he put in charge of hardware; Avie Tevanian, who headed up software; and David Manovich, who was put in charge of sales. Jobs has a reputation as a micromanager, but at NeXT he had learned to trust these lieutenants. He no longer oversees every decision the way he used to. At Pixar, Jobs delegated almost everything to Catmull and Lasseter. At Apple, Jobs cedes much of the day-to-day management to Tim Cook, the chief operating officer, a master at operations and logistics who is widely considered the number two at Apple. When Jobs took six weeks' sick leave in 2005 after his cancer operation, Cook took over as acting CEO. Ron Johnson, head of retail, manages almost everything to do with Apple's chain of retail stores; while chief financial officer Peter Oppenheimer handles finances and deals with Wall Street. Delegation at Apple frees up Jobs to do what he loves best—develop new products.

Jobs's Job

Working with partners like Jonathan Ive and Jon Rubinstein, Jobs plays a unique role. He doesn't design circuit boards or write code, but Jobs puts his stamp firmly on his teams' work. He's the leader who provides the vision, guides the development, and makes many of the key decisions. "He didn't create anything really, but he created everything," wrote former CEO John Sculley on Jobs's contribution to the original Mac.

According to Sculley, Jobs once said to him: "The Macintosh is inside of me, and I've got to get it out and turn it into a product."[12]

Jobs acts as the team director, the arbiter who rejects or accepts the work of his creative partners, guiding them as they work toward a solution. One source told me that Ive once confided that he wouldn't be able to do the work he does without Jobs's input. Ive may be a creative genius, but he needs Jobs's guiding hand.

Jobs is the "product picker," in the parlance of Silicon Valley. A product picker is a term used by Silicon Valley venture capitalists to identify the key product person at startup companies. By definition, a startup must succeed on its first product. If it doesn't, it goes under. But not all startups start with a product. Some startups are a group of engineers who have a lot of talent and ideas, but haven't yet figured out what product they want to develop. This happens all the time in the Valley, but to ensure the success of a startup like this, there has to be an individual who's got a nose for what that product should be. It's not always the CEO or a top executive, and they may not have expertise in management or marketing: their skill is picking out the key product from a torrent of ideas.

"The products bubble up but there has to be a czar," explained Geoffrey Moore, a venture capitalist and technology consultant. Moore is the author of *Crossing the Chasm*, the best-selling book about bringing high-tech products to the mainstream that is revered as Silicon Valley's marketing bible. "The success or failure of a startup depends on its first product," continued Moore. "It's a hits business. Startups must have a hit or they'll fail. If you pick the right product you win big."[13]

Moore said Jobs is the consummate product picker. One of the key things Moore looks for in pitch meetings when startups are looking for venture capital is the fledgling company's product picker. Picking products doesn't work by committee— there has to be an individual who is able to act as a decision maker.

General Motor's vice chairman Bob Lutz, the legendary "car czar," is a good example. An ex-Chrysler, Ford, and BMW executive, Lutz is famous for a string of distinctive, design-driven hit cars like the Dodge Viper, Plymouth Prowler, and BMW 2002. He's a quintessential "car guy" who knocks out distinctive vehicles rather than the designed-by-committee look-alikes of competitors. Ron Garriques, a former Motorola executive responsible for the hit Razr mobile phone, is another example. In 2007, Garriques was recruited by Michael Dell—newly returned to his troubled company—to run Dell's consumer business, and pick hit products, no doubt.

"It's a high-wire act," said Moore. "It's very clear when you fail. You have to risk everything every time you do it. It's playing center court at Wimbledon. And you have to have a lot of power to do it. Not many have the power or the will to push it through [the] organization without being edited or compromised or watered down. It doesn't work if you pick by committee."

At Apple, Jobs has successfully picked and guided to

development a hit product every two or three years—the iMac, the iPod, the MacBook, the iPhone. "Apple is a hit-driven company," said Moore. "It's had one hit after another."

For much of the last century, there were myriad companies run by similar strong-willed product czars, from Thomas Watson Jr. at IBM to Walt Disney. But the number of successful companies with product czars at the helm, like Sony under Akio Morita, has dwindled in recent years. Many contemporary companies are run by committee. "What's missing today is that these kind of entrepreneurs are no longer there," lamented Dieter Rams, the design genius who helped propel Braun to prominence for several decades. "Today there is only Apple and to a lesser extent Sony."[14]

Pugilistic Partners

During product development, Jobs is involved in many major decisions, from whether there should be fans for cooling machines to the font used on the box. But although Jobs is king of the mountain, the decision making at Apple isn't all top down. Argument and debate are central to Jobs's creative thinking. Jobs wants partners who challenge his ideas, and whose ideas can be challenged by him, often forcefully. Jobs makes decisions by engaging in hand-to-hand intellectual combat. It's demanding and pugnacious, but rigorous and creative.

Take the pricing of the first Mac in 1984. Jobs wrestled the pricing of the Mac with Sculley for several weeks. Not a couple of meetings. They argued about the issues night and day for *weeks*. The pricing of the Mac presented a big problem. Apple's revenues were on the slide, and the Mac had been expensive to develop. Sculley wanted to recoup the R&D investment, and he wanted to raise enough money to strategically out-advertise the competition. But if the Mac was priced too high, it might scare off buyers and wouldn't sell in volume. Both men took turns debating the opposing side of the argument—the thesis and antithesis—playing devil's advocate to see where the arguments would lead. Sculley euphemistically called arguing with Jobs "jousting." "Steve and I enjoyed taking one position, then turning it around and adopting another argument," Sculley wrote. "We would constantly joust over what each of us thought about new ideas, projects and colleagues."

There was likely similar "jousting" at Apple when the iPhone was launched in the summer of 2007. The iPhone initially cost $600, but within two months of its release, Jobs had dropped the price to $400. There were howls of protests from early adopters, who rightly felt ripped off. The outcry was so vociferous, Jobs issued a rare public apology and a $100 rebate.

Jobs dropped the iPhone's price because the initial response had exceeded Apple's expectations—it had sold more than one million units—and Jobs saw an opportunity to rapidly ramp up sales in the crucial holiday period. For a lot of consumer electronics, including the iPod, there are as many sales during the holiday period as there are the rest of the year. "iPhone is a breakthrough product, and we have the chance to 'go for it' this holiday season," Jobs wrote in a note to customers on the Apple website. "iPhone is so far ahead of the competition, and now it will be affordable by even more customers. It benefits both Apple and every iPhone user to get as many new customers as possible in the iPhone 'tent.' "

Day to day at Apple, meetings with Jobs can often be arguments—long, combative arguments. Jobs relishes intellectual combat. He wants a high-level discussion—even a fight—because it's the most effective way to get to the bottom of a problem. And by hiring the best people he can find, he ensures the debate is at the highest possible level.

A meeting with Jobs can be a trial by fire. He'll challenge everything that is said, sometimes extremely rudely. But it's a test. He is forcing people to stick up for their ideas. If they feel strongly enough, they'll defend their position. By raising the stakes, and people's blood pressures, he's testing to see if they know their facts and have a strong argument. The more firmly they stand, the more likely they're right. "If you're a yes-man you're doomed with Steve because he's pretty confident about what he knows, so he needs someone to challenge him," ex-Apple programmer Peter Hoddie told me. "Sometimes he says, 'I think we need to do this'—and it's a test to see if anyone will challenge him. These are the kinds of people he's looking for."[15]

It's extremely difficult to bullshit Jobs. "If you don't know what you're talking about, he's going to find out," said Hoddie.

"He's really bright. He's extremely well informed. He has access to some of the best people on the planet. If you don't know what you're talking about, he's gonna know."

Hoddie described one occasion when he was arguing with Jobs about some new chip technology under development at Intel, the processor supplier. Occasionally, Hoddie would bullshit Jobs just to get him off his back. Later that day, Jobs cornered Hoddie and challenged him about his earlier statements about Intel. Jobs had phoned up Intel's chairman, Andy Grove, and asked him about the technology Hoddie had been talking about. Luckily, Hoddie hadn't been bullshitting. "You can't bluff someone who can pick up the phone and talk to Andy," Hoddie said, laughing.

During his thirty-year career, Jobs has maintained a string of creative partnerships, beginning with his high school buddy Steve Wozniak. The list includes the original Mac design team, from the hardware genius Burrell Smith to programming luminaries such as Alan Kay, Bill Atkinson, and Andy Hertzfeld. In the decade Jobs has been working with design genius Jonathan Ive, Apple has led the world in industrial design. His partners at Apple include Jon Rubinstein, who oversaw a string of hit hardware, from the iMac to the iPod; and Ron Johnson, who masterminded Apple's retail stores, one of the most successful moneymaking chains ever (more on the stores later). And at Pixar, his teaming with Ed Catmull and John Lasseter created a moviemaking powerhouse.

"Think Different"

One of Jobs's most productive working partnerships has been with Lee Clow, a tall, bearded hippie adman and his agency, TBWA/Chiat/Day. Jobs's partnership with Clow and his agency has spanned several decades and produced some of advertising's most memorable and influential campaigns, from the 1984 TV spot that introduced the Macintosh, to the iPod silhouette ads plastered across billboards worldwide.

Headquartered in Los Angeles, TBWA/Chiat/Day is considered one of the most creative advertising companies in the world. Cofounded in 1968 by Guy Day, an L.A. ad veteran, and Jay Chiat, a hard-driving New Yorker who relocated to sunny Southern California in the mid-1960s, the company is now run by its longtime creative director Lee Clow. The company was once considered "gonzo" for its controversial, sometimes reckless, approach to advertising, but has matured and now boasts sober, blue-chip clients such as Nissan, Shell, and Visa.

For Apple the company has produced widely acclaimed, award-winning campaigns that are often regarded more as cultural events than mere advertising blitzes. Ads like "Think Different," "Switchers," and "I'm a Mac" have been widely discussed, critiqued, parodied, and copied. When a campaign spawns hundreds of parodies on YouTube and is turned into a sketch on late-night comedy shows, then the ads have graduated from the commercial to the cultural realm.

Jobs's association with the ad company began in the early

1980s, when the agency—then known as Chiat/Day—was producing a series of popular ads for Apple's computers. In 1983, the agency began work on what would become one of the most celebrated ads in advertising history: the TV commercial that introduced the Macintosh during the third quarter of the Super Bowl in January 1984.

The spot began with a tag line taken from another, discarded ad: "Why 1984 won't be like '1984' "—a reference to George Orwell's dystopian novel. It was too good a line to just throw away, so the agency pitched it to Apple. And, of course, it was perfectly suited for the launch of the Mac. The agency hired British director Ridley Scott, who'd just finished filming *Blade Runner*, to film the ad on a London soundstage. Using a cast of British skinheads, Scott portrayed a bleak Orwellian future, where a Big Brother squawking propaganda from a giant TV cows the masses into submission. Suddenly, in rushes an athletic woman in a Macintosh T-shirt, who smashes the screen with the toss of a sledgehammer. The sixty-second spot never showed the Mac, nor any computer, but the message was clear: the Mac would free downtrodden computer users from the hegemony of IBM.

Apple's board of directors was shown the spot just a week before it was due to air and freaked out. They ordered the ad pulled from the Super Bowl, but Chiat/Day was unable to sell the slot in time and the ad ran.

It turned out to be fortuitous: the ad garnered more attention and more press than the game itself. Although it was shown only twice (during the Super Bowl and earlier, on an obscure TV station in the middle of the night to make it eligible for advertising awards), the ad was rebroadcast in countless news reports and on *Entertainment Tonight*. Apple estimated that more than 43 million people saw the ad, which was worth millions of dollars in free advertising, according to an estimate by then-CEO John Sculley.

"The commercial changed advertising; the product changed the ad business; the technology changed the world," wrote *Advertising Age* columnist Bradley Johnson in a 1994 retrospective. "It turned the Super Bowl from a football game into advertising's Super Event of the year and it ushered in the era of advertising as news."[16]

The "1984" ad is typical of Jobs. It was bold and brash, and unlike any other commercial of its time. Instead of a straightforward product presentation, "1984" was a mini-movie with characters, a narrative, and high production values. Jobs didn't think of it, write it, or direct it, but he was smart enough to team up with Lee Clow and Jay Chiat, and give them the room to be creative.

The "1984" ad went on to win at least thirty-five awards for Chiat/Day, including the Grand Prix at Cannes, and generated millions of dollars in new commissions and clients. It also ushered in an era of lifestyle advertising that downplayed a product's features in favor of its appeal. No one else was thinking about advertising in the same way, especially in the computer industry; and very few companies were willing to communicate with the public in such an original, unorthodox way. Jobs left Apple in 1985 and the company switched agencies not long after his departure. But when Jobs returned in 1996, he brought back the agency to create a campaign that would "refocus" Apple.

Jobs was concerned about Apple's lack of focus, and asked Chiat/Day to create a campaign that would speak to Apple's core values. "They asked us to come in and talk about what Apple needed to do to get its focus back," Clow said. "It really wasn't hard; it was just to go back to Apple's roots."[17]

Clow, who's habitually dressed in T-shirt, shorts, and sandals, said the idea for "Think Different" came from thinking about the Mac user base—the designers, artists, and creatives who remained loyal customers through the company's darkest days. "Everybody immediately embraced the idea that this campaign should be about being creative and thinking out of the box," Clow said. "It got bigger when we said why not celebrate anyone who's ever thought about ways that they could change the world, and that's when Gandhi and Edison started coming into the conversation."[18]

The campaign came together very quickly and featured a series of black-and-white photos of about forty famous iconoclasts, including Muhammad Ali, Lucille Ball and Desi Arnaz, Maria Callas, Cesar Chavez, Bob Dylan, Miles Davis, Amelia Earhart, Thomas Edison, Albert Einstein, Jim Henson, Alfred Hitchcock, John Lennon and Yoko Ono, the Reverend Martin Luther King Jr., Rosa Parks, Picasso, Jackie Robinson, Jerry

Seinfeld, Ted Turner, and Frank Lloyd Wright. Apple ran the ads in magazines and billboards, and aired a TV ad celebrating "the misfits, the rebels, the troublemakers … the crazy ones."

"The people who are crazy enough to think they can change the world are the ones that do," the ad proclaimed.

The commercial came at a critical time in Apple's history. The company needed a public statement of its values and its mission: as much for its employees as for its customers. The "Think Different" campaign trumpeted Apple's virtues: its creativity, its uniqueness, and its ambitions. Again, it was a big, bold statement—Apple was associating itself, and its users, with some of humankind's most celebrated leaders, thinkers, and artists.

The photos were run without identifying labels, a strategy previously used by the agency for a 1984 Nike campaign featuring famous athletes. The lack of labels challenged the viewer to figure out who the subject was. This strategy makes the ads inclusive and involving. It rewarded those in the know. If you knew who the ad featured, it saluted you as an insider, part of the cognoscenti.

Jobs was involved from the beginning, submitting personal heroes like Buckminster Fuller and Ansel Adams. He also used his extensive contacts and formidable persuasive powers to secure permissions from the likes of Yoko Ono, John Lennon's widow, and the estate of Albert Einstein. But he declined the agency's suggestion to feature Jobs himself in one of the ads.

Out-advertise the Competition

Advertising has always been extremely important to Jobs, second only to the technology. Jobs's long-stated ambition is to make computers accessible to all, which to him means they have to be advertised to the public. "My dream is that every person in the world will have their own Apple computer. To do that, we've got to be a great marketing company," he has said.[19] Jobs is immensely proud of Apple's advertising. He often debuts new ads during his Macworld keynote speeches. If he's giving a product presentation, there's usually an ad to accompany the new product, and Jobs always shows it off to the public. If the ad is particularly good, he'll show it twice, obviously delighted.

More than anyone else in the PC industry, Jobs has strived to create a unique, non-nerdy image for computers. In the late 1970s, Jobs hired Regis McKenna, a Silicon Valley advertising pioneer, to help make Apple's early machines appeal to ordinary consumers. The advertising had to communicate to consumers why they needed one of these new PCs. There was no inherent demand for home computers: the ads would have to create it. McKenna drafted colorful ads showing computers in domestic settings. The ads were written in simple, easy-to-understand language, with none of the technical jargon that dominated competitors' ads, who, after all, were trying to appeal to a completely different market—hobbyists.

The first magazine ad for the Apple II shows a preppy young man playing with the machine on a kitchen table, while his wife, washing the dishes, looks on adoringly. The ad's sexual politics may have been old-fashioned, but it conveyed a message that Apple's PCs were useful, utilitarian machines. The kitchen setting made them seem like just another labor-saving appliance.

The importance of advertising to Jobs is clearly illustrated by his choice of CEO to run Apple in its early days: John Sculley, a marketing executive from PepsiCo who had used advertising to build Pepsi into a Fortune 500 company. Sculley was Apple's CEO for ten years, and though he made some strategic mistakes, he was stunningly successful at using marketing to grow Apple. When he took over in April 1983, Apple had $1 billion in revenues. It was a $10 billion company when he left a decade later.

In 1983, Apple was one of America's fastest growing companies, but it needed an experienced executive to manage growth. Just twenty-six, Jobs was judged by Apple's board to be too young and inexperienced to handle the job himself, so Jobs spent many months finding an older executive he could work with.

He chose Sculley, the thirty-eight-year-old president of PepsiCo, who'd masterminded the "Pepsi Generation" advertising campaign, which helped unseat Coke as the number-one brand for the first time in its history. Jobs spent several months courting Sculley, an experienced executive and a marketer extraordinaire, to run the company.

During the "Cola Wars" of the '70s, Sculley massively boosted Pepsi's market share by spending huge sums of cash on savvy TV advertising. Expensive, slick campaigns like the "Pepsi Challenge" transformed Pepsi from an underdog into a soda giant on equal footing with Coca-Cola. Jobs wanted Sculley to apply the same advertising chops to the fledgling market for personal computers. Jobs was especially worried about the Macintosh, which would debut in a few months. Jobs felt that advertising would be one of the major factors in its success. He wanted the Mac to appeal to the general public—not just electronics freaks—and advertising a weird and unfamiliar new product would be key to that. Sculley had no technology experience whatsoever, but it didn't matter. Jobs wanted his marketing expertise. Jobs wanted to create an "Apple Generation."

Sculley ran Apple in partnership with Jobs. He became Jobs's mentor and teacher, applying his marketing expertise to the nascent but rapidly growing PC market. Sculley and Jobs's strategy at Apple was to build sales rapidly and then out-advertise the competition. "Apple hadn't yet realized that as a billion-dollar corporation it had immense advantages we hadn't exploited," Sculley wrote in his autobiography, *Odyssey*. "It's almost impossible for a company with sales of $50 million or even $200 million to invest in the kinds of effective television advertising campaigns you need if you're going to leave any impression at all."[20]

Jobs and Sculley immediately boosted Apple's advertising budget from $15 million to $100 million. Sculley said their goal was to make Apple "first and foremost a product marketing company." Many critics have dismissed Apple's advertising flair, rejecting it as trivial and unimportant. Pure flash; no substance. But at Apple, marketing has always been one of its key strategies. Apple has used advertising as an extremely important and effective way to distinguish itself for the competition. "Steve and I were convinced we had the secret formula—a combination of revolutionary technology and marketing," wrote Sculley.[21]

Sculley's ideas have been very influential on Jobs, laying the groundwork for many of Jobs's marketing techniques at Apple today.

At PepsiCo, Sculley was responsible for some of the earliest and most successful examples of lifestyle advertising— emotionally charged spots that tried to reach people's minds through their hearts. Rather than try to market specific attributes of Pepsi over other sodas, which were negligible, Sculley created advertising that articulated an "enviable lifestyle."

Sculley's "Pepsi Generation" ads featured wholesome American kids engaged in idealized leisure pursuits: playing with puppies in a field or eating watermelon at a picnic. They portrayed uncomplicated vignettes of life's magic moments, set in a mythical middle America. They were designed to appeal to baby boomers—the fastest-growing, wealthiest consumers in the post–World War II economy—by portraying a lifestyle they'd aspire to. They were the first "lifestyle" ads.

The Pepsi commercials were treated like miniature movies, shot with the highest production values by Hollywood filmmakers. When other companies were spending $15,000 to shoot a commercial, Pepsi spent between $200,000 and $300,000 for a single spot.[22]

Jobs does exactly the same thing at Apple today. Apple is famous for its lifestyle advertising. It never loads its ads with speeds and feeds, functions and features, like everyone else. Instead, Apple engages in lifestyle marketing. It portrays hip young people with "enviable lifestyles," given to them courtesy of Apple's products. Apple's highly successful iPod ad campaign shows young people grooving to the music in their heads. There is never any mention of the iPod's hard drive capacity.

Sculley also perfected big splashy marketing events, like Macworld, as news. Sculley dreamed up the "Pepsi Challenge"— a blind taste test that pitted Pepsi against Coke, staged at grocery stores, malls, and big sports events. These challenges often caused such a splash that they would often attract local TV crews. A spot on the local TV news that evening was worth far more than any thirty-second commercial. Sculley upped the stakes: organizing celebrity challenges at big sports games that would often garner massive publicity. "Marketing, after all, is really theater," Sculley wrote. "It's like staging a performance. The way to motivate people is to get them interested in your product, to entertain them, and to turn your product into an incredibly important event. The Pepsi Generation campaign did all this in scaling Pepsi to epic proportions and making a brand bigger than life."[23]

Jobs uses the same technique to introduce new products at the annual Macworld Expo. Jobs has turned his trademark "one more thing" keynote speeches at Macworld into massive media events. They are marketing theater, staged for the world's press.

One More Thing:
Coordinated Marketing Campaigns

The Macworld speech is just one part of much bigger, coordinated campaigns that are executed with a precision that would impress a general. The campaigns combine rumor and surprise with traditional marketing, and rely wholeheartedly on secrecy for their effectiveness. On the outside it can look somewhat chaotic and uncontrolled, but they are tightly planned and coordinated. Here's how it works.

Weeks ahead of a secret product announcement, Apple's PR department sends out invitations to the press and VIPs. The invitation gives the time and location of a "special event" but contains scant information about its nature or any upcoming products that might be revealed. It's a tease. Jobs is effectively saying, "I've got a secret, guess what it is."

Immediately, tongues start wagging. There'll be an explosion of blog posts and press articles speculating on what Jobs will announce. In years past, the speculation was limited to specialist Apple websites and fan forums, but more recently the mainstream press also reports the rumors. The *Wall Street Journal*, the *New York Times*, CNN, and the *International Herald Tribune* have all written breathless articles looking forward to Jobs's product presentations. The rumor-mongering surrounding Macworld 2007—where Jobs introduced the iPhone—even made the nightly news on all the cable and TV networks, which is unheard of for any company in any industry. Not even Hollywood can garner as much attention for its movie premieres.

This kind of worldwide publicity is worth many hundreds of millions of dollars in free exposure. The launch of the iPhone in January 2007 was the biggest to date. Standing onstage in San Francisco, Jobs single-handedly eclipsed the much larger Consumer Electronics Show in Las Vegas, which was happening at the same time. The CES is more important economically than Macworld, yet Jobs and the iPhone handily stole its thunder. Jobs's iPhone launch also overshadowed announcements from much bigger companies, including the introduction of the consumer version of Microsoft's Vista, and became the biggest technology story of the year. Harvard Business School professor David Yoffie estimated that the iPhone rumor reports and follow-up stories were worth $400 million in free advertising. "No other company has ever received that kind of attention for a product launch," Yoffie says. "It's unprecedented."[24]

It was so successful that Apple didn't spend a penny to advertise the iPhone before its launch. "Our secret marketing program for the iPhone was none," Jobs told Apple employees in a companywide address. "We didn't do anything."

Of course, there wouldn't be this kind of attention if the product plans were known ahead of time. The whole stunt relies on secrecy, which is tightly enforced. At San Francisco's Moscone Center, the Apple booth is shrouded in a twenty-foot-high black curtain. The curtain's only entrance, at the back, is manned by a guard who carefully checks the credentials of all who try to enter. Two more guards are stationed at opposing corners of the rectangular booth, monitoring the sides. Everything inside the curtain is also wrapped, including the tops of the display stands. Even the main presentation stage, which sits in the center of the booth, is completely wrapped with fabric on all sides. All the advertising banners hanging from the ceiling are wrapped on all sides. The banner wrappings have elaborate pulley mechanisms to remove the curtains after Jobs makes his announcement. There are big banner ads upstairs at the entrance, which are also wrapped in black canvas. The banners are protected 24/7 by guards. One year, the guards caught some bloggers taking pictures and forced them to erase their memory cards. "The urge to clamp down on information sometimes borders on paranoia," wrote Tom McNichol in *Wired* magazine.

Several weeks before launch, Apple's PR department sends the new gadget under strict nondisclosure agreements to three of the most influential technology product reviewers: Walt Mossberg at the *Wall Street Journal*, David Pogue at the *New York*

Times, and Edward Baig at *USA Today*. It's always the same three reviewers, because these three have proven track records of making and breaking products. A bad review can doom a device, but a good one can make it a blockbuster. Mossberg, Pogue, and Baig prepare their reviews for publication on the product's launch date.

Meanwhile, Apple's PR department contacts the national news and business magazines offering a behind-the-scenes "making of" peek at the product. This "making of" is usually anything but—most details are withheld—however, it's better than nothing and the magazines always take Jobs up on it. Putting Jobs's face on the cover moves magazines on the newsstands. Jobs plays off old rivalries. He pits *Time* against *Newsweek* and *Fortune* against *Forbes*. The magazine that promises the most extensive coverage gets the exclusive. Jobs uses this same trick time after time, and it always gets results. Jobs started this practice with the original Mac and called them "sneaks," as in sneak peeks. Familiarizing a reporter with a new product ahead of time usually guaranteed a more favorable review. When Jobs launched a new iMac in 2002, *Time* magazine got the exclusive behind-the-scenes story, and in return Jobs got the front cover and a glossy seven-page spread inside. It was timed perfectly for the machine's introduction at Macworld.

During the speech, he always saves the biggest announcement for last. At the end, he'll say there's "one more thing," almost as though it were an afterthought.

The minute Jobs unveils the product, Apple's marketing

machine begins its advertising blitz. The secret banners at Macworld are unveiled, and immediately the front door of Apple's website showcases the new product. Then begins a coordinated campaign in magazines, newspapers, radio, and TV. Within hours, new posters go up on billboards and bus stops all over the country. All the ads reflect a consistent message and styling. The message is simple and direct: "One thousand songs in your pocket" is all you need to know about the iPod. "You can't be too thin. Or too powerful" sends a clear message about Apple's MacBook laptops.

The Secret of Secrecy

Jobs's Apple is obsessively secretive. It's almost as secretive as a covert government agency. Like CIA operatives, Apple employees won't talk about what they do, even with their closest confidants: wives, boyfriends, parents. Employees certainly will not discuss their work with outsiders. Many won't even refer to the company by name. Like superstitious theater folk who call *Macbeth* the "Scottish play," some Apple employees call it "the fruit company."

Talking out of school is a firing offense. But many employees don't know anything anyway. Apple staffers are given information on a strictly need-to-know basis. Programmers write software for products they've never seen. One group of engineers designs a power supply for a new product, while another group works on the screen. Neither group gets to see the final design. The company has a cell structure, each group isolated from the other, like a spy agency or a terrorist organization.

In the old days, the information flowed so fast out of Apple that the legendary trade publication *MacWeek* was known as MacLeek. Everyone, from engineers to managers, was feeding information to the press. Since Jobs's return, Apple's 21,000 employees as well as dozens of suppliers are extremely tight-lipped. Despite dozens of reporters and bloggers sniffing around, very little good information leaks out about the company's plans or upcoming products.

In January 2007, a judge ordered Apple to pay the $700,000 in legal fees of two websites that reported details of an unreleased product code-named "Asteroid." Apple had sued the sites in an attempt to learn the identity of the person in its ranks who leaked the information, but lost the case.

Some speculated that Jobs sued the websites to keep the press in line. The lawsuit was seen as press intimidation, a scare tactic designed to intimidate the press from reporting rumors. Much of the public discussion concerned press freedom and whether bloggers have the same rights as professional reporters, who enjoy some protection under laws that shield journalists. This is why the Electronic Frontier Foundation took on the case and turned it into a cause célèbre—to protect press freedom. But from Jobs's point of view, the case had nothing to do with press freedom. He sued the bloggers to scare the shit out of his own employees. He was less concerned with gagging the press than gagging staff who leaked to the press—

and anyone who might think of doing it in the future. Apple's buzz marketing is worth hundreds of millions of dollars, and Jobs wanted to check the leaks.

Some of Jobs's secrecy measures get a little extreme. When Jobs hired Ron Johnson from Target to head up Apple's retail effort, he asked him to use an alias for several months lest anyone get wind that Apple was planning to open retail stores. Johnson was listed on Apple's phone directory under a false name, which he used to check into hotels.

Apple's head of marketing, Phil Schiller, said he's not allowed to tell his wife or kids what he's working on. His teenage son, an avid iPod fan, was desperate to know what his dad was cooking up at work, but Daddy had to keep his trap shut lest he get canned. Even Jobs himself is subject to his own strictures: he took an iPod hi-fi boombox home for testing, but kept it covered with a black cloth. And he listened to it only when no one else was around.

Apple's obsessive secrecy is not a quirk of Jobs's control-freak tendencies; it's a key element of Apple's extremely effective marketing machine. Apple makes millions of dollars in free advertising every time Jobs steps onto a stage to reveal a new product. Many have wondered why there are no bloggers at Apple. It's because loose lips at Apple sink ships. But there are dozens of bloggers at Pixar, even before Jobs sold Pixar to Disney. Pixar bloggers happily gossip about all aspects of Pixar's projects and their work lives. The difference is that Pixar's movies don't rely on a surprise unveiling to get press. New movies are routinely reported in the Hollywood trade press. Jobs isn't a control freak for the sake of it; there's a method to his madness.

Personality Plus

Jobs has been very successful at creating a persona for Apple. Through advertising, he has shown the public the things he, and Apple, stands for. In the late 1970s, it was revolution through technology. Later it was about being creative, thinking different. Jobs's personality allows Apple to market itself as human, and cool. His personality is the raw material of Apple's advertising. Even an agency like Chiat/Day could never ever make Bill Gates look cool.

Apple's advertising has done a good job at conveying the company as an icon of change, of revolution, and of bold thinking. But it does so in a subtle, indirect way. Apple rarely brags. It never says, "We're revolutionary. Really." It uses the storytelling of its advertising to convey this message, often as a subtext.

Take the iPod silhouette ads. The imagery of the campaign was fresh and new; it didn't look like anything that came before. "They always have this freshness in graphic design. The look is very simple and very iconic. It's so distinctive that it has a look to itself," advertising journalist Warren Berger, author of *Advertising Today* and *Hoopla*, told me in a telephone interview.[25]

Berger said the best way to get creative advertising is to hire the most creative agency. Chiat/Day is one of a handful of the most creative agencies in the world, but the real trick is to communicate what the brand is about. "Lee Clow and Jobs understood each other so well, they became buddies," said Berger. "Clow really got the culture of Apple, the mind-set. He really understood what they were trying to do. And Jobs gave Clow total creative freedom. He allowed Clow to show him anything no matter how crazy it might seem. It really allows people to push the boundaries. IBM could never do that. They would never give Chiat/Day the freedom that Jobs gave them."

In 2006, Hewlett-Packard started to do very good advertising, with campaigns that featured people, not computers, in spots that looked like they may have come from Apple. In one of HP's "The Computer Is Personal Again" TV spots, the hip-hop star Jay Z shows viewers the contents of his computer, which is conjured up as a 3D special effect between his gesticulating hands. His face is never shown.

Hewlett-Packard hired Goodby Silverstein, another superstar agency. The ads were interesting and very well done, but they never had the strength of personality of Apple's ads, because *the company* doesn't have the strength of personality. No matter how the ads tried to personalize HP the corporation through celebrities like Jay Z, it still felt like a company. Apple is more of a phenomenon than a company. Hewlett-Packard can never be quite as magical because it doesn't have a personality. The same thing happened to Apple when Jobs left in 1985. "When Steve left, Apple became a company again," said Berger.

"The advertising was good, but it didn't have that magic. It didn't look like the same company. It wasn't a phenomenon. It didn't feel like a revolution. It was just trying to stabilize things."

Between the big, bold, brand-building campaigns, like "Think Different" and the iPod silhouettes, Apple mixes in more traditional product advertising. These product promotions focus on specific products, like the "I'm a Mac/I'm a PC" campaign, which dramatized why it makes sense to buy an Apple computer.

The campaigns represented the rival Mac and Windows platforms as two people. Up-and-coming actor Justin Long personified the effortlessly cool Mac, while comedian and author John Hodgeman represented the nerdy, accident-prone PC. In one spot, Hodgeman has a cold. He's contracted a virus. He offers Long, the Mac, a handkerchief, which he politely declines because Macs are largely immune to computer viruses. In thirty seconds, the spot cleverly and economically conveyed a message about computer viruses. The ads create a memorable, dramatic situation—more so than HP's individuals showing the contents of their computer.

Like "Think Different," the campaign had a big impact. It enjoyed a high profile and was widely parodied—a good measure of a campaign's cultural impact.

"They create this stuff that gets into the culture," said Berger. "Soon enough people are talking about it, and he gets into others' advertising. You see the same layouts, the same motifs, in other ads, in magazine and newspaper layouts. There's a whole graphic design look; suddenly other advertisers have embraced it. The 'Think Different' posters. People put them on their wall. That's really successful advertising. The ads became a phenomenon. You didn't have to pay people to pass it around."

Not everyone loves Apple's advertising. Seth Godin, author of several best-sellers about marketing, said Apple's advertising has often been mediocre. "I'm underwhelmed by most of Apple's advertising," he told me by phone from his office in New York. "It's not been effective. Apple's advertising is more about pandering to the insiders than acquiring new users. If you have a Mac, you love Apple's advertising because it says 'I'm smarter than you.' If you don't have a Mac it says 'you're stupid.'"[26]

The "I'm a Mac/I'm a PC" ads have been described as unbearable smug. Many critics couldn't stand Justin Long's self-consciously hip Mac character, who had the poise and self-assurance that annoys some people. The stubble and a casual hoodie added to the irritation. Many in the target audience identified more with Hodgeman's nebbish PC character, who was endearingly bumbling.

"I hate Macs," wrote British comedian Charlie Booker in a critique of the ads. "I have always hated Macs. I hate people who use Macs. I even hate people who don't use Macs but sometimes wish they did.... PCs have charm; Macs ooze pretension. When I sit down to use a Mac, the first thing I think is,

'I hate Macs', and then I think, 'Why has this rubbish aspirational ornament only got one mouse button?' "

Booker said the campaign's biggest problem is that it "perpetuates the notion that consumers somehow 'define themselves' with the technology they choose."

He continues, "If you truly believe you need to pick a mobile phone that 'says something' about your personality, don't bother. You don't have a personality. A mental illness, maybe— but not a personality."[27]

Conversely, the "Switchers" campaign, which ran in the early 2000s, was ripped for portraying Apple customers as losers. The campaign, shot by Oscar-winning documentarian Errol Morris, featured a series of ordinary people who had recently switched from Windows computers to Macs. Looking straight into Morris's camera, they explained the reasons they switched, the problems they had been having with Windows, and rhapsodized their new love affair with the Mac. Trouble was, most seemed like they were running away from their problems. They couldn't cope, and they had given up.

"Apple couldn't have picked a starker collection of life's losers with which to promote the Macintosh," wrote journalist Andrew Orlowski.[28] "The message is a mass of conflicting signals. Having portrayed the Mac as the computer for overachievers, it's now suggesting that it's a kind of refugee camp for life's most bitter losers."

The "Think Different" campaign was criticized for using noncommercial figures, people who patently didn't believe in commercial culture. It even included committed nonmaterial-ists like Gandhi and the Dalai Lama, who actively opposed commercialism. These figures would never endorse a product in a commercial—and here Apple was using them to endorse products. A lot of critics couldn't believe Apple's chutzpah and thought the company had stepped over the line.

In Apple's defense, Clow told the *New York Times* that Apple intended to honor the subjects of the campaign, not exploit them. "We're not trying to say these people use Apple, or that if they could've used a computer, they would've used Apple. Instead, we're going for the emotional celebration of creativity, which should always be part of how we speak about the brand."[29]

Allen Olivio, an Apple spokesperson at the time, said: "We would never associate these people with any product; it's Apple celebrating them versus Apple using them. To say that Albert Einstein would have used a computer would cross the line. Why would he need one? But it's different to say he looked at the world differently."[30]

Berger, the ad critic, said he loved the "Think Different" campaign. "American culture is very commercial. This stuff gets jumbled up. Quentin Tarantino talks about Burger King. Apple makes a poster of Rosa Parks. That's our culture. People are free to use anything from wherever they want."

Lessons from Steve:

- *Partner only with A players and fire bozos.* Talented staff are a competitive advantage that puts you ahead of your rivals.
- *Seek out the highest quality*—in people, products, and advertising.
- *Invest in people.* When Jobs axed products after returning to Apple, he "steved" a lot of projects, but he kept the best people.
- *Work in small teams.* Jobs doesn't like teams of more than one hundred members, lest they became unfocused and unmanageable.
- *Don't listen to "yes" men.* Argument and debate foster creative thinking. Jobs wants partners who challenge his ideas.
- *Engage in intellectual combat.* Jobs makes decisions by fighting about ideas. It's hard and demanding, but rigorous and effective.
- *Let your partners be free.* Jobs gives his creative partners a lot of rope.

Chapter 5

Passion: Putting a Ding in the Universe

"I want to put a ding in the universe."

—Steve Jobs

At every turn of his career, Steve Jobs has inspired employees, lured software developers, and snagged customers by invoking a higher calling. For Jobs, programmers don't work to make easy-to-use software; they're striving to change the world. Apple's customers don't buy Macs to work on spreadsheets; they're making a moral choice against the evil monopoly of Microsoft.

Take the iPod. It's a cool MP3 player. It's a great blend of hardware, software, and online services. It's driving Apple's comeback. But for Jobs, it's primarily about enriching people's lives with music. As he told *Rolling Stone* in 2003: "We were very lucky—we grew up in a generation where music was an incredibly intimate part of that generation. More intimate than it had been, and maybe more intimate than it is today, because today there's a lot of other alternatives. We didn't have video games to play. We didn't have personal computers. There's so many other things competing for kids' time now. But, none-theless, music is really being reinvented in this digital age, and that is bringing it back into people's lives. It's a wonderful thing. And in our own small way, that's how we're working to make the world a better place."[1]

Get that last part: "that's how we're working to make the world a better place." In everything Jobs does, there's a sense of mission. And like any true believer, he's passionate about his work. Yes, his commitment produces a lot of screaming and shouting. Jobs is no pussycat when dealing with underlings. He knows what he wants, and he'll throw a fit to get it. Oddly, many of his collaborators like getting yelled at. Or at least, they like the effect it has on their work. They appreciate his passion. He pushes them to greatness, and, though they might burn out, they learn a lot along the way. Jobs's secret: it's OK to be an asshole, as long as you're passionate about it.

Making the world a better place has been Jobs's mantra from the get-go. In 1983, Apple was six years old and grow-ing explosively. It was transforming from a classic Silicon Val-ley startup run by young hippies into a big corporation with blue-chip customers. It needed a seasoned businessman in charge.

Jobs had spent months trying to seduce John Sculley, the president of PepsiCo, to run the company. But Sculley wasn't convinced it was wise to step down as head of a big established firm for a risky, hippie startup like Apple. Still, Sculley was tempted. Personal computers were the future. The pair met numerous times in Silicon Valley and New York. Finally, one evening, looking out over Central Park from the balcony of Jobs's luxury apartment at the San Remo building, Jobs turned to the older man and brazenly challenged him: "Do you want to sell sugar water for the rest of your life, or do you want to change the world?"

It's perhaps the most famous challenge in modern business history: it's an insult, a compliment, and a soul-searching, philosophical challenge rolled into one question. Of course, the question cut Sculley to the core. It unsettled him profoundly, and he fretted about it for days. In the end, he couldn't resist the gauntlet Jobs had thrown down. "If I didn't accept, I'd have spent the rest of my life wondering if I made the wrong decision," Sculley told me.

Ninety Hours a Week and Loving It

The team that developed the first Mac was a ragtag bunch of ex-academics and technicians working on an under-the-radar skunkworks affair that had little chance of seeing the light of day—until Jobs took it over. Right from the get-go, Jobs convinced the team that they were creating something revolutionary. This wasn't just a cool computer or a challenging engineering problem. The Mac's easy-to-use graphical interface was going to revolutionize computing. For the first time, computers would be accessible to the nontechnical public.

The Mac team members worked like slaves for three years, and though Jobs screamed at them, he kept up morale by instilling in them the conviction that they had a higher calling. The work they were doing was nothing less than God's work. "The goal was never to beat the competition, or to make a lot of money; it was to do the greatest thing possible, or even a little greater," wrote Andy Hertzfeld, one of the lead programmers.

Jobs told the Mac team they were artists, fusing technology with culture. He convinced them that they were in a unique position to change the face of computing, and privileged to be designing such a groundbreaking product. "For a very special moment, all of us have come together to make this new product," Jobs wrote in an essay for the premier issue of *Macworld* magazine in 1984. "We feel this may be the best thing we'll ever do with our lives."

In retrospect, this turned out to be true. The Mac was a revolutionary breakthrough in computing. But this was perhaps an article of faith. The Mac was just one of dozens of competing computers being developed at the time. There was no guarantee it would be better, or even that it would get released to market. The team took Jobs's conviction on faith. They joked that their belief in Jobs's vision was the same kind of faith instilled by leaders of charismatic cults.

But Jobs instilled in his team a passion for their work, which is critical when trying to invent new technologies. Without it, workers might lose faith in a project that takes several years to come to fruition. Without a passionate commitment to their work, they might lose interest and abandon it. "Unless you have a lot of passion about this, you're not going to survive," Jobs has said. "You're going to give it up. So you've got to have an idea or a problem or a wrong that you want to right that you're passionate about; otherwise you're not going to have the perseverance to stick it through. I think that's half the battle right there."

Jobs's passion is a survival strategy. Many times when Jobs and Apple have tried something new, there have been a few true believers, but the wider world's reaction has often been disdainful. In 1984, the first Mac's graphical user interface was widely derided as "a toy." Bill Gates was mystified that people wanted colored computers. Critics initially called on Apple to open up the iPod. Without a strong belief in his vision, a passion for what he was doing, it would be much harder for Jobs to resist the critics. "I've always been attracted to the more revolutionary changes," Jobs told *Rolling Stone*. "I don't know why. Because they're harder. They're much more stressful emotionally. And you usually go through a period where everybody tells you that you've completely failed."

Instilling employees with a passion for what the company is doing has a very practical application: staffers are generally happy to work extremely long hours, even by Silicon Valley's workaholic standards. The Mac team worked long, hard hours because Jobs made them believe the Mac was their product. It was their creativity and work that was bringing the product to life, and he made them believe they would have a profound impact. What better motivator is there? At Apple, technology is a team sport. The Mac development team worked so hard that it became a badge of honor. They all got sweatshirts emblazoned with "90 HOURS A WEEK AND LOVING IT."

The Hero/Asshole Rollercoaster

Many of Apple's staff genuinely believe that Apple is making a dent in the universe. They strongly feel that Apple is leading technology, setting trends, and breaking new ground. To be part of that is very enticing. "People do believe that Apple is changing the world," said one former staff member. "Not everyone believes it 100 percent, but they all believe it at least a little. As an engineer, what Apple is doing is very exciting. There was always something exciting about to happen. The company has incredible momentum."

At Apple, the corporate culture trickles down from Jobs. Just as Jobs is exceedingly demanding of the people who report to him, Apple's middle managers demand the same level of high performance from their staff. The result is a reign of terror. Everyone is in constant fear of losing their jobs. It's known as the "hero/asshole rollercoaster." One day you're a hero, the next you're an asshole. At NeXT, Jobs's employees called it the "hero/shithead rollercoaster." "You live for days when you're a hero and try to get through the days when you're an asshole," said a former staffer. "There's incredible highs and there's incredible lows."

According to several staffers I talked to, there's a constant tension at Apple between the fear of getting fired and a messianic zeal for making a dent in the universe. "More than anywhere else I've worked before or since, there's a lot of concern about being fired," explained Edward Eigerman, a former Apple engineer. "You'd ask your coworkers, 'Can I send this e-mail, or file this report?' People would say, 'you can do whatever you want on your last day at Apple.'"[2]

Eigerman spent four years at Apple working as an engineer in a New York sales office. Everyone he worked with eventually got fired for one reason or another, he said, mostly for performance-related issues, like not meeting their numbers. But on the other hand, no one quit either. Even though working at Apple was demanding and stressful, everyone loved their job and was extremely loyal to the company and to Steve Jobs.

"People love to work there," said Eigerman. "They are very excited to be there. There's a lot of passion. People love the products. They really believe in the products. They are very excited about what they are doing."

Despite the zeal, employees are distinctly un-cultish. They consciously avoid the cultish types. At a job interview, the worst thing a prospective employee can say is: "I've always wanted to work at Apple," or "I've always been a big fan." That's the last thing Apple employees want to hear. Staffers like to describe each other as "level-headed."

The stress of riding the hero/asshole rollercoaster would be intolerable if a lot of staffers weren't giddy to work at Apple. As well as wanting to put a ding in the universe, several employees described other perks of working at Apple, including the high caliber of fellow employees, an outstanding corporate cafeteria, and the challenge of working on the cutting edge of technology.

A Wealth of Stock Options

One of the best perks is Apple's employee stock options, which have become very valuable as Apple's stock has surged a split-adjusted 1,250 percent since Jobs returned as CEO in 1997, according to *Business Week*. At Apple, there are few corporate indulgences. Jobs has his own personal Gulfstream V jet, but most officers and executives fly coach. There are no generous expense accounts. The lavish retreats of Apple's early days—where hundreds of salespeople would be entertained at a Hawaiian resort for a week—are long gone.

But most of Apple's full-time employees have grants of stock options, which are awarded to them when they join the company. After a vesting period, usually a year, staffers are allowed to buy chunks of stock at a discounted price, typically the price of the stock when they were first hired. When they sell the stock, the difference between the purchase price and the selling price is kept as profit. The higher the stock rises, the more money they make. Stock options are a popular form of employee compensation in the technology industry. It's non-cash compensation, which makes it cheap to issue, and it more or less guarantees that employees have to work like slaves to raise the stock price.

Engineers, programmers, managers, and other mid-level staffers who make up the majority of Apple's payroll are typically awarded several thousand stock options. At 2007 prices, several thousand stock options could be worth anywhere between $25,000 to $100,000—or considerably more, depending on the stock price and the employee's vesting schedule.

Higher-level managers and executives have much larger grants. In October 2007, Apple's senior vice president of retail, Ron Johnson, cashed in 700,000 shares worth about $130 million before taxes. According to regulatory filings with the Securities and Exchange Commission, Johnson exercised the options at about $24, and immediately sold them for about $185 apiece. In 2005, Johnson made about $22.6 million on stock options, and in 2004, $10 million according to reports.

Apple also has a popular stock purchase plan. Employees can buy discounted stock in chunks based on their salary. The stock is priced at the lowest price in the last six months, plus a percentage discount, which is guaranteed to make a little money, and quite often a lot of money. I received reports of Apple staff buying fancy cars, making down payments on houses, and salting large sums of cash in the bank.

"At Apple we gave all our employees stock options very early on," Jobs told *Fortune* in 1998. "We were among the first in Silicon Valley to do that. And when I returned, I took away most of the cash bonuses and replaced them with options. No cars, no planes, no bonuses. Basically, everybody gets a salary and stock.... It's a very egalitarian way to run a company that Hewlett-Packard pioneered and that Apple, I would like to think, helped establish."

Indeed, Apple did help establish stock options as standard Silicon Valley compensation procedure. During the boom, options became the norm at companies all across the tech sector. So important were options that, on returning to Apple in 1997, Jobs immediately fought hard to reprice plunging options to prevent an exodus of staff to other companies. As *Time* magazine reported that August: "To restore morale, Jobs says, he went to the mat with the board to lower the price of incentive stock options. When the board members resisted, he pushed for their resignations."

Later, Jobs got into trouble with his own stock options, a situation that hadn't been resolved at the time of this writing. In 2006, the Securities and Exchange Commission launched a widespread investigation into more than 160 companies, including Apple and Pixar, that had allegedly backdated stock options. According to the SEC, companies were routinely repricing options to a date prior to the actual date the options were granted—usually when the stock price was lower, which boosted the worth of the stock. Backdating options is not technically illegal, but improperly reporting backdated options is, and, according to the SEC, it was widespread.

In the early 2000s, Jobs was awarded two big stock option grants that were backdated, according to the SEC. In June 2006, Apple launched an internal investigation headed by two board members: former U.S. vice president Al Gore and former IBM and Chrysler chief financial officer Jerry York. In December 2006, Gore and York issued a report that found "no misconduct" by Jobs, although the report admitted Jobs knew about some of the backdating. However, Jobs didn't realize the accounting implications, the report said. The report laid the blame for backdating on two officers no longer with the company, who were later identified as former general counsel Nancy Heinen and former CFO Fred Anderson. In December, Apple restated earning and took a $84 million charge. Shareholders sued the company, but the suit was dismissed in November 2007.

Because of repeated stock option grants, employees who have been at Apple for many years have a lot of money tied up in the company. For most staff, there is no better motivator to protect the company's interests. As a result, several employees told me that they are happy to march in lockstep and zealously enforce the rules. One source, who declined to be named, said he'd happily snitch out colleagues who leaked product plans to the press. The staffer pointed to the Engadget blog, which reported a rumor in 2006 that the iPhone would be delayed. The false rumor caused a 2.2 percent dip in Apple's stock—knocking $4 billion off the market cap. "I've got a vested interest in stopping that kind of crap," the employee said.

Likewise, Eigerman said he knows that there is someone inside Apple who is sending tips and pictures to an Apple rumor website. He doesn't know the tipster's name, but he is mystified why anyone would risk their job, and possibly criminal or civil lawsuits, to send product plans and pictures to a website. It's unlikely they're getting paid for the information. "It's very strange to me," said Eigerman. "The risk is enormous. Who would do that? The psychology is very strange to me."

Dangling the Carrot and the Stick

Jobs uses both the carrot and the stick to get his team to produce great work. He's uncompromising, and the work has to be of the highest standard. He sometimes insists on things that are seemingly impossible, knowing that eventually even the thorniest problem is solvable. John Sculley was impressed with Jobs's powers of persuasion: "Steve provided phenomenal inspiration and demanding standards to get his team to do such things," Sculley wrote. "He pushed them to their limits, until even they were amazed at how much they were able to accomplish. He possessed an innate sense of knowing exactly how to extract the best from people. He cajoled them by admitting his own vulnerabilities; he rebuked them until they, too, shared his uncompromising ethic; he stroked them with pride and praise, like an approving father."[3]

Sculley described how Jobs would celebrate the team's accomplishments with "unusual flair." He uncorked bottles of champagne to mark milestones, and frequently treated the team to educational trips to museums or exhibits. He'd spring for lavish, bacchanalian "retreats" at expensive resorts. To celebrate Christmas 1983, Jobs threw a black-tie party in the main ballroom of San Francisco's posh St. Francis Hotel. The team waltzed the night away to the strains of Strauss played by the San Francisco Symphony. He insisted the team sign the inside of the Mac's case, the way that artists sign their work. When the Mac was finally finished, Jobs presented each member with his or her own machine bearing a personalized plaque. In recent years, he's expanded his largess to the entire company, or at least, to all the full-time staff. He's given iPod Shuffles to all Apple employees, and, in 2007, all of Apple's 21,600 full-time employees got a complimentary iPhone.

Yet Jobs can also be extremely cutting and cruel. There are numerous accounts of Jobs's calling employees' work "a piece of shit" and throwing it at them in a rage. "I was amazed at his behavior even when the criticism was correct," said Sculley.[4] "He was constantly forcing people to raise their expectations of what they could do," Sculley told me. "People were producing work that they never thought they were capable of, largely because Steve would shift between being highly charismatic and motivating. He'd get them excited, to feel like they are part of something insanely great. But on the other hand, he would be almost merciless in terms of rejecting their work until he felt it had reached the level of perfection that was good enough to go into this case, the Macintosh."[5]

One of the Great Intimidators

Jobs is one of the "great intimidators," a category of fearsome business leaders characterized by Roderick Kramer, a social psychologist at Stanford. According to Kramer, great intimidators inspire people through fear and intimidation, but aren't mere bullies. They're more like stern father figures, who inspire people through fear as well as through a desire to please. Other examples include Miramax's Harvey Weinstein, Hewlett-Packard's Carly Fiorina, and Robert McNamara, the U.S. secretary of defense during the Vietnam War. Great intimidators tend to be clustered in industries with high risks and high rewards: Hollywood, technology, finance, and politics.

Most management advice for the last twenty-five years has focused on issues like empathy and compassion. Advice books encourage building teamwork through kindness and understanding. There's been very little written about scaring the pants off employees to improve results. But as Richard Nixon said, "People react to fear, not love—they don't teach that in Sunday School, but it's true."

Like other great intimidators, Jobs is forceful. He pushes and cajoles, often quite hard. He can be brutal and ruthless. He's willing to use "hard power"—to put the fear of God into people—to get things done. This kind of leadership is most effective in crisis situations, like company turnarounds, when someone needs to take the reins and make sweeping changes. But as Jobs has shown, it's very effective in getting products to market—quickly. Kramer found that many business leaders aspire to such power. Yes, they treat employees with fairness and compassion, and they may be well liked, but every now and again they'd love to be able to put boot to ass to get things done.

Jobs often puts boot to ass and has often stepped over the line, especially when he was younger. Larry Tessler, Apple's former chief scientist, said Jobs inspired equal measures of fear and respect. When Jobs left Apple in 1985, people in the company had very mixed feelings about it. "Everybody had been terrorized by Steve Jobs at some point or another and so there was a certain relief that the terrorist would be gone," Tessler said. "On the other hand, I think there was incredible respect for Steve Jobs by the very same people, and we were all worried what would happen to this company without the visionary, without the founder, without the charisma."[6]

Some of it is pure show. Jobs has chewed out underlings in public for the effect it has on the rest of the organization. General George S. Patton used to practice his "general's face" in the mirror. Reggie Lewis, an entrepreneur, also admitted to perfecting a scowl in the mirror for use in hardball negotiations. Contrived anger is common among politicians, and has been called "porcupine anger," Kramer reports.

Jobs possesses a keen political intelligence, what Kramer calls "a distinctive and powerful form of leader intelligence." He's a good judge of character. He assesses people, coolly and clinically, as instruments of action, ways of getting things done.

Kramer described a job interview conducted by Mike Ovitz, the fearsome Hollywood agent who built the Creative Artists Agency into a powerhouse. Ovitz sat the interviewee in the blinding afternoon sunlight and kept calling in his secretary to give her instructions. Ovitz had set up the constant interruptions beforehand to test the interviewee. He wanted to keep them on their toes and see how they handled distractions. Jobs does the same thing: "Many times in an interview I will purposely upset someone: I'll criticize their prior work. I'll do my homework, find out what they worked on, and say, 'God, that really turned out to be a bomb. That really turned out to be a bozo product. Why did you work on that?...' I want to see what people are like under pressure. I want to see if they just fold or if they have firm conviction, belief, and pride in what they did."[7]

One senior HR executive from Sun once described for *Upside* magazine an interview with Jobs. She'd already endured more than ten weeks of interviews with senior Apple executives before reaching Jobs. Immediately, Jobs put her on the spot: "He told me my background wasn't suitable for the position. Sun is a good place, he said, but 'Sun is no Apple.' He said he would have eliminated me as a candidate from the start."

Jobs asked the woman if she had any questions, so she queried him about corporate strategy. Jobs dismissed the question: "We're only disclosing our strategy on a 'need-to-know' basis," he told her. So she asked him why he wanted an HR executive. Big mistake. Jobs replied: "I've never met one of you who didn't suck. I've never known an HR person who had anything but a mediocre mentality." Then he took a telephone call, and the woman left a wreck.[8] If she had stuck up for herself, she would have fared much better.

Take, for example, an Apple saleswoman who received a public tongue lashing from Jobs at one of the company's annual sales meetings. Every year, several hundred of Apple's sales reps gather for a few days, typically at Apple's Cupertino HQ. In 2000, about 180 reps were sitting in Apple's Town Hall auditorium waiting for a pep talk from their leader. Apple had just announced its first loss in three years. Immediately, Jobs threatened to fire the entire sales team. Everyone. He repeated the threat at least four times during the hour-long talk. He also singled out the female sales executive who dealt with Pixar— his other company at the time—and in front of everyone he laid into her: "You are not doing a good job," he bellowed. Over at Pixar, his other job, he had just signed a $2 million sales order with Hewlett-Packard, one of Apple's rivals, he said. The Apple rep had been competing for the contract, but lost out. "He called this woman out in front of everyone," Eigerman recalled. But the saleswoman stood up for herself. She started yelling back. "I was very impressed with her," Eigerman said. "She was furious. She defended herself but he would not hear her out. He told her to sit down. The saleswoman is still at Apple, and she is doing very well…. It's the asshole/hero roller-coaster."

Perhaps most significantly, the public humiliation of the unfortunate rep put the fear of God into all the other sales reps. It sent a clear message that everybody at Apple is held personally accountable.

Two years later at the annual sales meeting, Jobs was extremely pleasant and courteous. (He skipped the 2001 sales meeting, which was held off-site.) Jobs thanked all the sales reps for doing a great job and took questions for half an hour. He was genuinely very nice. Like other intimidators, Jobs can be immensely charming when he needs to be. Robert McNamara had a reputation for being cold and distant, but he could turn on a dazzling spotlight of charm when he wanted to. "Great intimidators can also be great ingratiators," Kramer writes.

Jobs is famous for his reality distortion field—a ring of charisma so strong that it bends reality for anyone under its influence. Andy Hertzfeld encountered it soon after joining the Mac development team: "The reality distortion field was a confounding melange of a charismatic rhetorical style, an indomitable will, and an eagerness to bend any fact to fit the purpose at hand. If one line of argument failed to persuade, he would deftly switch to another. Sometimes, he would throw you off balance by suddenly adopting your position as his own, without acknowledging that he ever thought differently. Amazingly, the reality distortion field seemed to be effective even if you were acutely aware of it, although the effects would fade after

Steve departed. We would often discuss potential techniques for grounding it, but after a while most of us gave up, accepting it as a force of nature."

Alan Deutschman, a Jobs biographer, fell under Jobs's spell at their first meeting. "He uses your first name very often. He looks directly in your eyes with that laser-like stare. He has these movie-star eyes that are very hypnotic. But what really gets you is the way he talks—there's something about the rhythm of his speech and the incredible enthusiasm he conveys for whatever it is he's talking about that is just infectious. At the end of my interview with him, I said to myself, 'I have to write an article about this guy just to be around him more—it's so much fun!' When Steve wants to be charming and seductive, no one is more charming."[9]

Working with Jobs: There's Only One Steve

Thanks to his fearsome reputation, many staffers try to avoid Jobs. Several employees, past and present, told essentially the same story: keep your head down. "Like many people, I tried to avoid him as much as possible," said one former employee. "You want to stay below his radar and avoid him getting mad at you." Even executives try to stay out of Jobs's way. David Sobotta, a former director of Apple's federal sales, describes how he once went to the executive floor to pick up a vice president for a briefing. "He quickly suggested a route off the floor that didn't go in front of Steve's office," Sobotta wrote on his website. "He explained the choice by saying it was safer."[10]

In return, Jobs keeps a distance from rank-and-file employees. Except with other executives, he is fairly private at Apple's campus. Kramer writes that remaining aloof instills a mixture of fear and paranoia that keeps employees on their toes. Staff are always working hard to please him, and it also allows him to reverse decisions without losing credibility.

But it's not always easy to avoid Jobs. He has a habit of dropping in on different departments unannounced and asking people what they're working on. Every now and then Jobs praises employees. He doesn't do it too often, and he doesn't go overboard. His approval is measured and thoughtful, which amplifies the effect because it is rare. "It really goes to your head because it's so hard to get it out of him," said one employee. "He's very good at getting to people's egos."

Of course, the desire to avoid Jobs is not universal. There are plenty of employees at Apple only too eager to get Jobs's attention. Apple has its full share of aggressive, ambitious staffers keen to get noticed and promoted.

Jobs is often the center of workplace conversation. The subject of Steve comes up a lot. He gets credit for everything that goes right at Apple, but he also gets blamed for everything that goes wrong. Everyone's got a story. Employees love to discuss his outbursts and his occasional quirks.

Like the Texan billionaire Ross Perot, who banned beards

among his employees, Jobs has some idiosyncrasies. One former manager who had regular meetings in Jobs's office kept a pair of canvas sneakers under his desk. Whenever he was called for a meeting with Jobs, he'd take off his leather shoes and put on the sneakers. "Steve is a militant vegan," the source explained.

Inside the company, Jobs is known simply as "Steve" or "S.J." Anyone else whose name is Steve is known by their first and last names. At Apple, there is only one Steve.

There are also F.O.S.—Friends Of Steve—persons of importance who are to be treated with respect and sometimes caution: you never know what might get reported. Staffers warn each other about F.O.S.s to be careful around. Friends Of Steve are not necessarily in Apple's upper management tier—sometimes they are fellow programmers or engineers who have a connection.

Under Jobs, Apple is a very flat organization. There are few levels of management. Jobs has an exceptionally wide-ranging knowledge of the organization—who does what and where. Though he has a small executive management team—just ten officers—he knows hundreds of the key programmers, designers, and engineers in the organization.

Jobs is quite meritocratic: he's not concerned with formal job titles or hierarchy. If he wants something done, he generally knows whom to go to and he contacts them directly, not through their manager. He's the boss, of course, and can do things like that, but it shows his disdain for hierarchies and formalities. He'll just pick up the phone and call.

Critics have compared Jobs to a sociopath without empathy or compassion. Staff are inhuman objects, mere tools to get things done. To explain why employees and coworkers put up with him, critics invoke the Stockholm Syndrome. His employees are captives who have fallen in love with their captor. "Those who know anything much about his management style know he works by winnowing out the chaff—defined as those both not smart enough and not psychologically strong enough to bear repeated demands to produce something impossible (such as a music player where you can access any piece of music within three clicks) and then be told that their solution is 'shit.' And then hear it suggested back to them a few days later," wrote Charles Arthur in *The Register*. "That's not how most people like to work, or be treated. So in truth, Steve Jobs isn't an icon to any managers, apart from the sociopathic ones."

As far as great sociopathic managers go, Jobs is relatively mild, at least now that he's entered middle age. Other intimidators, like moviemaker Harvey Weinstein, are much more abrasive. Larry Summers, the former dean of Harvard, who forced through a series of reforms at the university, conducted infamous "get to know you sessions" with faculty and staff that started with confrontation, skepticism, and hard questioning, and went downhill from there. Jobs is more like a demanding, hard-to-please father. It's not just fear and intimidation. Underlings work hard to get his attention and his approval. A former Pixar employee told Kramer that he dreaded letting Jobs down, the same way he dreaded disappointing his father.

Many people who work for Jobs tend to burn out, but in hindsight they relish the experience. During his research, Kramer said he was surprised that people who worked with great intimidators often found the experience "profoundly educational, even transformational." Jobs works people hard and heaps on the stress, but they produce great work. "Did I enjoy working with Steve Jobs? I did," Cordell Ratzlaff, the Mac OS X designer, told me. "It was probably the best work I did. It was exhilarating. It was exciting. Sometimes it was difficult, but he has the ability to pull the best out of people. I learned a tremendous amount from him. There were high points and there were low points but it was an experience." Ratzlaff worked directly with Jobs for about eighteen months, and said it would have been hard staying on any longer than that. "Some people can stick it out for longer than that. Avie Tevanian, Bertrand Serlet. I've seen him screaming at both of them, but they had some way of weathering that. There have been cases, people who have been with him for a very, very long time. His admin worked with him for many, many years. One day, he fired her: 'That's it, you're not working here anymore,'" Ratzlaff said.

After nine years working at Apple, the last few closely with Jobs, programmer Peter Hoddie ended up quitting, somewhat acrimoniously. Not because he was burned out, but because he wanted more control at Apple. He was tired of getting his orders from Jobs and wanted to have a greater say in the company's plans and products. They had a fight, Hoddie quit, but later Jobs was contrite. He tried to talk Hoddie out of leaving. "You're not going to get away that easy," Jobs said to Hoddie. "Let's talk about this." But Hoddie stuck to his guns. On his last day, Jobs called him from his office across campus. "Steve was charming to the end," Hoddie said. "He said good luck. It wasn't, 'fuck you.' Of course, there's a degree of calculation in everything he does."

Lessons from Steve

- *It's OK to be an asshole, as long as you're passionate about it.* Jobs screams and shouts, but it comes from his drive to change the world.
- *Find a passion for your work.* Jobs has it, and it's infectious.
- *Use the carrot and the stick to get great work.* Jobs praises and punishes as everyone rides the hero/asshole rollercoaster.
- *Put boot to ass to get things done.*
- *Celebrate accomplishments with unusual flair.*
- *Insist on things that are seemingly impossible.* Jobs knows that eventually even the thorniest problem is solvable.
- *Become a great intimidator.* Inspire through fear and a desire to please.
- *Be a great ingratiator as well as an intimidator.* Jobs turns on the spotlight of charm when he needs to.
- *Work people hard.* Jobs heaps on the stress, but staffers produce great work.

Chapter 6

Inventive Spirit: Where Does the Innovation Come From?

"Innovation has nothing to do with how many R&D dollars you have. When Apple came up with the Mac, IBM was spending at least 100 times more on R&D. It's not about money. It's about the people you have, how you're led, and how much you get it."

—Steve Jobs, in *Fortune*, November 9, 1998

On July 3, 2001, Apple put its critically praised Power Mac G4 Cube on ice. Jobs had introduced the cube-shaped machine just a year before, to critical raves. An eight-inch cube of translucent plastic that popped CDs from its top like a toaster, the Cube was a smash hit with critics. The *Wall Street Journal*'s Walt Mossberg said it was "simply the most gorgeous personal computer I've ever seen or used." Jonathan Ive won several awards for its design. But it was not a hit with consumers. It sold poorly. Apple had hoped for sales of 800,000 the first year, but shifted less than 100,000 units. A year after its introduction, Jobs suspended production of the machine and issued an unusual press release.[1] "The company said there is a small chance it will reintroduce an upgraded model of the unique computer in the future, but that there are no plans to do so at this time," the release said. It appeared Jobs couldn't bear to discontinue the Cube officially, but he wasn't prepared to sell any more either. It was sent to a permanent product purgatory.

The Cube was Jobs's baby: a beautifully designed, technically advanced machine that represented months, maybe years, of prototyping and experimentation. The Cube packed a lot of powerful hardware into a very tight space. It was fast and capable, and dispensed completely with one of Steve Jobs's oldest pet peeves—an internal cooling fan. But aside from a few design museums, few were interested in it. At about $2,000, it was too expensive for most consumers, who wanted a cheap monitor-less Mac like the Mac mini that succeeded it. And those who could afford it—creative professionals who worked in graphics or design—needed a more powerful machine that could be easily upgraded with new graphics cards or extra hard drives. They bought the cheaper Power Mac G4 tower instead. It was ugly, but it worked.

Jobs had badly misjudged the market. The Cube was the wrong machine at the wrong price. In January 2001, Apple reported a quarterly loss of $247 million, the first since Jobs had returned to the company. He was stung.

The Cube was one of Jobs's few missteps since returning to Apple, and he learned a valuable lesson from it. The Cube was one of the few products he's overseen that was entirely design led. It was an experiment in form over function. The cube has always been one of Jobs's favorite forms. The computer he sold at NeXT—the NeXT Cube—was a pricey, laser-cut cube made of magnesium (which, funnily enough, was also a market failure). The underground Apple store on Manhattan's Fifth Avenue is topped by a giant glass cube that Jobs helped to design (which is not a failure). *The Register* called the G4 Cube a "glorious experiment of aesthetics over commonsense."[2] Instead of focusing on what customers wanted, Jobs thought he could give them an elegant museum piece, and it cost him.

Jobs usually pays very careful attention to the customer experience. It's one of the things that has earned him a reputation for innovation. One of the central questions about Jobs and Apple is: Where does the innovation come from? Like any complex phenomenon, it comes from many places, but much of it is informed by Jobs's careful attention. From the scroll wheel on the iPod to the box the iPod comes in, Jobs is alert to every aspect of the customer experience. His instinct for the experience of using his products is what drives and informs Apple's innovation, and the Cube was one of the rare occasions when he took his eye off the ball.

An Appetite for Innovation

One of the hottest topics in business these days is innovation. With ever-increasing competition and shortening product cycles, companies are desperate to find the magic key to innovation. In the search for a system, workers are sent to innovation workshops where they play with Legos to unleash their creativity. Companies are hiring chief innovation officers, or opening innovation centers where managers brainstorm, free associate, and "ideate" surrounded by boxes of Legos.

Jobs is scornful of such ideas. At Apple there is no system to harness innovation. When asked by Rob Walker, a *New York Times* reporter, if he ever consciously thinks about innovation, Jobs responded: "No. We consciously think about making great products. We don't think, 'Let's be innovative! Let's take a class! Here are the five rules of innovation, let's put them up all over the company!'" Jobs said trying to systemize innovation is "like somebody who's not cool trying to be cool. It's painful to watch.... It's like watching Michael Dell try to dance. *Painful.*"[3]

Nonetheless, Jobs has an almost mystical reverence for innovation. As described earlier, his heroes are some of industry's greatest inventors and entrepreneurs: Henry Ford, Thomas Edison, and Edwin Land. Apple's former CEO, John Sculley, wrote that Jobs often spoke of Land. "Steve lionized Land, saw in him one of America's greatest inventors. It was beyond his belief that Polaroid ousted Land after the only major failure in Land's career—Polavision, an instant movie system that failed to compete against videotape recording and resulted in a near $70 million write-off in 1979. 'All he did was blow a lousy few million and they took his company away from him,' Steve told me with great disgust."[4]

Sculley recalled a trip he and Jobs took to see Land after he was kicked out of Polaroid. "He had his own lab on the Charles River in Cambridge," Sculley recalled. "It was a fascinating afternoon because we were sitting in this big conference room with an empty table. Dr. Land and Steve were both looking at the center of the table the whole time they were talking. Dr. Land was saying, 'I could see what the Polaroid camera should be. It was just as real to me as if it was sitting in front of me before I had ever built one.' And Steve said, 'Yeah, that's exactly the way I saw the Macintosh.' He said, 'If I asked someone who had only used a personal calculator what a Macintosh should be like, they couldn't have told me. There was no way to do consumer research on it. I had to go and create it and then show it to people and say, 'Now what do you think?' Both of them had this ability to—well, not invent products—but discover products. Both of them said these products have always existed, it's just that no one has ever seen them before. We were the ones who discovered them. The Polaroid camera always existed and the Macintosh always existed. It's a matter of discovery. Steve had huge admiration for Dr. Land. He was fascinated by that trip."

During television and magazine interviews, Jobs often invokes innovation as Apple's secret sauce. He's talked about innovation several times during his keynote speeches. "We are going to innovate ourselves out of this downturn," Jobs declared in 2001 when the PC industry was in recession. "Innovate," he boasted at Macworld Paris in September 2003. "That's what we do."

Under Jobs's leadership, Apple has earned a reputation as one of the most innovative companies in technology. *Business Week* in 2007 named Apple the most innovative company in the world, beating Google, Toyota, Sony, Nokia, Genentech, and a host of other A-list companies. It was the third year in a row that Apple had earned the top spot.[5]

Apple has brought to market a steady stream of innovations, including three of perhaps the most important innovations in modern computing: the first fully assembled personal computer, the Apple II; the first commercial implementation of the graphical user interface, the Mac; and, in 2001, the iPod—an Internet appliance for digital media disguised as a humble music player.

Apple produces blockbusters like the iMac, iPod, and iPhone, but there's also been a long list of smaller, yet important and influential products like the Airport, a line of easy-to-use WiFi base stations that enabled Apple's laptops to be among the first wireless notebooks, a trend that later went thoroughly mainstream, and the AppleTV, which links the TV in the living room with the computer in the den.

Apple has an unmatched reputation for innovation, but has historically been regarded as little more than an R&D lab for the rest of the PC industry. It may have created one innovation after another, but for many years it appeared unable to capitalize on its breakthroughs. Apple pioneered the graphical desktop, but Microsoft put it on 95 percent of the world's PCs. Apple invented the first PDA, the Newton, but Palm helped turn it into a $3 billion industry. While Apple innovated, companies like Microsoft and Dell made the big bucks. In this respect, Apple has been compared to Xerox PARC, the copier company's legendary research facility that more or less invented modern computing—the graphical desktop, Ethernet networking, and the laser printer—but failed to commercialize any of it. It was left to Apple to bring the graphical desktop to market, but it was Microsoft that really cleaned up.

Jobs, in fact, used to have a reputation for reckless innovation. He was so busy turning out the next groundbreaking product that he was unable to capitalize on the last one. Critics say he was charging ahead so fast, he recklessly failed to follow through on what he'd built. Take the Mac and the Apple II. By the mid-1980s, the Apple II was the PC industry's most successful computer, with a 17 percent market share in 1981. But when the Mac came out three years later, it was completely incompatible with the Apple II. The Mac didn't run Apple II software, and it didn't connect to Apple II peripherals. Developers couldn't easily port their Apple II software to the Mac—they had to do a complete from-the-bottom-up rewrite. And customers switching to the Mac had to start from scratch. They had to buy all new software and peripherals, at great expense. But Jobs wasn't interested in building on the Apple II's position of strength. He was interested in the future, which was graphical computing. "Jobs is a progenitor, not a nurse," wrote former Apple executive Jean Louis Gassée.[6]

Bill Gates never made these kinds of mistakes. Windows was built on top of Microsoft-DOS, and Office was built on top of Windows. Every version of Windows has been compatible with the preceding version. It's been slow, steady progress—and money in the bank.

Product vs. Business Innovation: Apple Does Both

Until recently, Jobs did not have much of a reputation for follow-through. For most of its history, Apple was seen as creative, but companies like Microsoft and Dell were the ones that executed. Pundits distinguished between companies like Apple, which are good at product innovation, and companies like Dell, which practice "business innovation." In the history of business, the most successful companies aren't product innovators, but those that develop innovative business models. Business innovators take the breakthroughs of others and build on them by figuring out new ways to manufacture, distribute, or market them. Henry Ford didn't invent the motorcar, but he did perfect mass production. Dell doesn't develop new kinds of computers, but it did create a very efficient direct-to-consumer distribution system.

But Jobs's reputation as a product genius without the ability to execute is unfair. The second time around at Apple, he's proven to be a master of execution. Since Jobs's return, Apple has been distinguished by superb execution—and orchestration—on all fronts: products, sales, marketing, and support.

For example, when Jobs took over in 1997, Apple was sitting on more than seventy days' worth of product inventory piled up in warehouses. In November 1997, Jobs launched an online store linked behind the scenes to a Dell-like, build-to-order manufacturing operation. "With our new products and our new store and our new build-to-order, we're coming after you, buddy," Jobs warned Michael Dell.

Within a year, Apple's inventory had been reduced from seventy days to one month. He recruited Tim Cook from Compaq to be Apple's new chief operating officer, and charged Cook with simplifying Apple's complex parts pipeline. At the time, Apple bought parts from more than one hundred different suppliers. Cook offshored most of Apple's manufacturing to contractors in Ireland, Singapore, and China. Most of Apple's portable products—the MacBooks, iPod, and iPhone—are now assembled by contractors based in mainland China. Cook dramatically reduced the number of basic component suppliers to about twenty-four companies.[7] He also persuaded parts suppliers to locate their factories and warehouses close to Apple's assembly plants, enabling an extremely efficient just-in-time manufacturing operation. In two years, Cook reduced inventory to six or seven days, where it remains today.

Apple these days runs the tightest ship in the computer industry. In 2007, AMR Research, a market research company, named Apple the number-two company in the world for supply chain management and performance, after Nokia. AMR measured several metrics related to execution, including revenue growth and inventory turns. "Apple's unparalleled demand-shaping capability lets its supply chain record spectacular results without sweating costs like everyone else," AMR said. Apple beat Toyota, Wal-Mart, Cisco, and Coca-Cola.[8] Dell didn't even make AMR's list.

Jobs loves to boast that Apple runs a tighter ship than Dell. "We beat Dell on operational metrics every quarter," Jobs told *Rolling Stone*. "We are absolutely as good of a manufacturer as Dell. Our logistics are as good as Dell's. Our online store is better than Dell's."[9] However, it should be noted that Apple sells half as many computers as Dell and has a much simpler product matrix.

Jobs has also developed his own share of innovative business models. Take the iTunes music store. Until Jobs persuaded the music labels to try selling songs individually for 99 cents, no one had found a formula for selling music online to compete with the illegal file-sharing networks. Since then, the iTunes music store has become the Dell of digital music.

And then there are Apple's retail stores, which are so unlike anything else in retailing, they've been called "experiential innovation." Modern retailing is all about the shopping experience, and Apple's low-key, friendly stores have added a new dimension to the experience of shopping for a computer (more on this later in the chapter).

Where Does the Innovation Come From?

Jobs appears to have an innate talent for innovation. It's as though ideas occur to him in a flash, a bolt from the blue. The light bulb goes on, and suddenly there's a new Apple product.

It's not quite like that. That's not to say there are no flashes of inspiration, but many of Jobs's products come from the usual sources: studying the market and the industry, seeing what new technologies are coming down the pipe and how they might be used. "The system is that there is no system," Jobs told *Business Week* in 2004. "That doesn't mean we don't have process. Apple is a very disciplined company, and we have great processes. But that's not what it's about. Process makes you more efficient."

He continued, "But innovation comes from people meeting up in the hallways or calling each other at 10:30 at night with a new idea, or because they realized something that shoots holes in how we've been thinking about a problem. It's ad hoc meetings of six people called by someone who thinks he has figured out the coolest new thing ever and who wants to know what other people think of his idea."[10]

Part of the process is Apple's overall corporate strategy: What markets does it target, and how does it target them? Part of it is keeping abreast of new technology developments and being receptive to new ideas, especially outside the company. Part of it is about being creative, and always learning. Part of it is about being flexible, and a willingness to ditch long-held notions. And a lot of it is about being customer-centric. Innovation at Apple is largely about shaping technology to the customer's needs, not trying to force the user to adapt to the technology.

Jobs's Innovation Strategy: The Digital Hub

The keynote speech Jobs gave at Macworld in San Francisco in January 2001 is remembered for the "one more thing" surprise ending: Jobs dropped the "i" from iCEO and became Apple's full-time leader. But earlier in his speech, Jobs laid out Apple's vision—a vision that would inspire more than a decade's worth of innovation at Apple, and would shape almost everything the company did, from the iPod to its retail stores and even its advertising.

The digital hub strategy is possibly the most important thing Jobs has laid out in a keynote speech. The idea, which seems somewhat obvious now, had far-reaching implications in almost everything Apple did. It shows how adherence to a simple, well-articulated idea can successfully guide corporate strategy, and influence everything from the development of products to the layout of retail stores.

Clean-shaven and dressed in a black turtleneck and blue jeans, Jobs began his speech by painting a rather bleak picture of the computer industry. He noted that the year 2000 had been a difficult year for Apple and the computer business as a whole. (In March 2000, the dot-com bubble began to burst, and purchases of computer equipment fell off a cliff.) Jobs showed the audience a slide of a gravestone inscribed with BELOVED PC, 1976–2000, R.I.P.

Jobs noted that many people in the computer industry were worried that the PC was waning, that its place at the center of things was over. But Jobs said the PC wasn't waning at all but was on the verge of its third great age.

The PC's first golden age, the age of productivity, started around 1980, with the invention of the spreadsheet, word processing, and desktop publishing. The golden age of productivity lasted almost fifteen years and drove the industry, Jobs said as he paced the Macworld stage. Then in the mid-1990s, the second golden age of the PC, the age of the Internet, began. "The Internet propelled the PC both in business and personal uses to new heights," Jobs noted.

But now, the computer was entering its third great age: the age of digital lifestyle, which was driven by an explosion of digital devices, Jobs said. He noted that everyone has cell phones, DVD players, and digital cameras. "We are living in a digital lifestyle with an explosion of digital devices," he said. "It's huge."

Most important, the computer was not peripheral to this digital lifestyle, Jobs argued, but at the very center of it. The computer was the "digital hub," the central docking station for all the digital devices. And by hooking digital devices to the computer, they became enhanced: the computer loaded music with an MP3 player, or edited video shot with a digital camcorder.

Jobs explained that he first began to understand the idea of a digital hub after Apple had developed iMovie, a video editing application. The iMovie application allows raw camcorder footage to be edited on the computer, which makes the camcorder much more valuable than it is alone. "It makes your camcorder worth ten times as much because you can convert raw footage into an incredible movie with transitions, cross dissolves, credits, soundtracks," Jobs said. "You can convert raw footage that you'd normally never look at again on your camcorder into an incredibly emotional piece of communication. Professional. Personal. It's amazing . . . it has ten times as much value to you."

This all seems obvious now, but at the time, few people were using their computers for such tasks, and it definitely wasn't mainstream. Jobs wasn't alone in recognizing that the computer was becoming a lifestyle device. Bill Gates had discussed the "digital lifestyle" the same week during his speech at the Consumer Electronics Show in Las Vegas. Intel CEO Craig Barrett was also giving speeches noting that the computer is "really the center of the digital world."

But Jobs's articulation amounted to a mission statement for Apple. The "digital hub" was the recognition of a major trend in the computer industry and a prescription for Apple's place in it. It allowed him to look at emerging technologies and consumer behavior, and formulate appropriate product strategies. (More on the digital hub in Chapter 7.)

Products as Gravitational Force

Part of the process at Apple is to focus on products, the end goal that guides and informs innovation. Wanton innovation is wasteful. There must be a direction, something to pull it all together. Some Silicon Valley companies develop new technologies and then go in search of problems for those technologies to solve. Take the Internet bubble of the late 1990s. The bubble was defined by this kind of thinking. It was a carnival of worthless innovation—half-baked business ideas pumped into vast money-burning concerns in a misguided attempt to get big quick and beat the competition. Entrepreneurs launched websites for selling pet food over the Net, or built giant warehouses for delivering groceries by van, before there was any inkling customers wanted to shop this way. And it turns out they didn't. No one wanted to get their groceries delivered from Webvan's automated warehouses. The Internet bubble burst, taking with it businesses that had developed solutions to problems that didn't exist.

"You need a very product-oriented culture, even in a technology company," Jobs said. "Lots of companies have tons of great engineers and smart people. But ultimately, there needs to be some gravitational force that pulls it all together."[11]

Jobs notes that before he returned, Apple had lost its product-oriented culture. In the late 1980s and early 1990s, there was great technology being developed in the company's labs, but there wasn't a product culture to put that technology to work. Instead, the company turned its focus to milking its key asset: the Mac user interface. Jobs noted that Apple had a monopoly on the graphical user interface for almost ten years, which sowed the seeds for its demise. Instead of trying to develop new, breakthrough products, the company concentrated on making maximum profit from its interface monopoly.

"The product people aren't the ones that drive the company forward anymore," Jobs said of Apple during that period. "It's the marketing guys or the ones who expand the business into Latin America or whatever. Because what's the point of focusing on making the product even better when the only company you can take business from is yourself?" Jobs said in situations like this, the people who built the company in the first place—the product-oriented staffers—tend to become replaced by those with a sales focus. "Who usually ends up running the show?" asked Jobs. "The sales guy."[12]

Jobs cited as a good example Steve Ballmer at Microsoft, the company's chief salesman who took over from Bill Gates, the programmer. "Then one day, the monopoly expires for whatever reason," Jobs continued. "But by then the best product people have left, or they're no longer listened to. And so the company goes through this tumultuous time, and it either survives or it doesn't." Luckily for Apple, it survived.

Pure Science vs. Applied Science

Money isn't the key to innovation. Apple spends a lot less than other companies on R&D, yet appears to get a lot more bang for its buck. Microsoft in 2006 spent more than $6 billion on R&D and is on track to spend $7.5 billion in 2007. Microsoft finances several large and well-funded research centers in Redmond, Silicon Valley, Cambridge in the UK, and China. There are some very impressive technologies being developed in Microsoft's research labs. The company boasts that it is leading research in speech recognition and fast search of massive databases. Each year, Microsoft gives journalists a tour of its Redmond research facility, and it is a treat for those invited to see all the cool toys and clever technologies the researchers are developing. But it is unclear how much of Microsoft's research is being directed toward its products. Except for speech recognition in Vista, which has been well received, there's little evidence that the labs are leading major new product initiatives. "You know, our friends up north spent over $5 billion on R&D, but these days all they seem to be copying is Google and Apple," Jobs said at Apple's World Wide Developers Conference in 2006. "Shows money doesn't buy everything."

In 2007, the management consultancy Booz Allen Hamilton released a study of worldwide corporate R&D spending and concluded that there's little evidence that increased R&D investment is linked to better results. "It's the process, not the pocketbook," Booz Allen concluded. "Superior results seem to be a function of the quality of an organization's innovation process—the bets it makes and how it pursues them—rather than either the absolute or relative magnitude of its innovation spending."

Booz Allen cited Apple as one of the thriftiest R&D spenders in tech, but one of the most successful. According to Booz Allen, Apple's 2004 R&D-to-Sales ratio was 5.9 percent, compared to an industry average of 7.6 percent. "Its $489 million spent is a fraction of its larger competitors," Booz Allen said. "But by rigorously focusing its development resources on a short list of projects with the greatest potential, the company created an innovation machine that eventually produced the iMac, iBook, iPod, and iTunes."[13]

Apple's R&D spending is like the old distinction between pure science and applied science. Pure science is the pursuit of knowledge for its own sake. Applied science is application of science to particular problems. Of course, pure science is extremely important, and will sometimes lead to the kind of fundamental breakthroughs that applied scientists don't even look at. But applied science, like engineering, is focused on more practical, pressing problems. The former head of Microsoft's research labs, Nathan Myhrvold, gained fame for academic papers he wrote about dinosaurs. He may have contributed to the field of paleontology, but did Microsoft invent the iPod?

Jobs uses as his inspiration Hewlett-Packard, one of the first Silicon Valley companies and one that has always had a strong engineering culture—it was driven by engineers who made products. "The older I get, the more I'm convinced that motives make so much difference," Jobs said. "HP's primary goal was to make great products. And our primary goal here is to make the world's best PCs—not to be the biggest or the richest." Jobs said Apple has a second goal, which is to make a profit—both to make money but also to keep making products. "For a time," Jobs said, "those goals got flipped at Apple, and that subtle change made all the difference. When I got back, we had to make it a product company again."[14]

The Seer—and Stealer

Jobs keeps his eyes peeled for promising new technologies, or existing technologies that Apple can improve, like early MP3 players or, lately, smart phones. Jobs has a reputation as a seer. He seems to have a magical ability to peer into the future and know before anyone else what consumers want. Jobs downplays his reputation as an oracle: "You can't really predict exactly what will happen, but you can feel the direction that we're going," Jobs told *Rolling Stone*. "And that's about as close as you can get. Then you just stand back and get out of the way, and these things take on a life of their own."[15]

Jobs has said he looks for "vectors going in time"—what new technologies are coming to market, which ones are ending their run. "You try to spot those things and how they're going to be changing over time and which horses you want to ride at any point in time," Jobs said. "You can't be too far ahead, but you have to be far enough ahead, because it takes time to implement. So you have to intercept a moving train."[16]

Jobs cited USB as an example. Intel invented the now-ubiquitous Universal Serial Bus (USB), and Apple was one of the first PC companies to build it into its computers. Jobs recognized its consumer-friendly potential: it wasn't fast, but it was plug and play, and it provided power to devices, eliminating an extra wire and power brick. It seems unremarkable now that USB is wildly popular, but Apple was one of the first companies to adopt it—and it may have never reached critical mass if it hadn't.

Innovation can—and often does—come from outside Apple. There's a long list of technologies that weren't developed at Apple that Jobs or his engineers recognized had innovative potential. WiFi wireless networking, developed by Lucent and Agere, didn't get much traction until Apple used it across its entire line of computers and built it into its Airport base stations, ushering in the era of wireless laptops.

Some observers note that innovation at Apple has less to do with inventing brand-new technologies than taking existing technologies and making them easy to use. Jobs takes technologies out of the lab and puts them in the hands of ordinary users.

The first and best example is the graphical user interface, which Jobs first spotted at age twenty-four in 1979, during a paid tour of Xerox's famed Palo Alto Research Center. During his visit, Jobs was given a demonstration of the Xerox Alto, the first computer with a mouse and point-and-click interface. "I thought it was the best thing I'd ever seen in my life. Now remember it was very flawed, what we saw was incomplete, they'd done a bunch of things wrong. But we didn't know that at the time but still thought they had the germ of the idea there and they'd done it very well and within you know ten minutes it was obvious to me that all computers would work like this some day."[17]

But Xerox's management had no idea what its scientists had cooked up in the lab. Despite dozens of demonstrations, Xerox's executives didn't see its potential. "Basically they were copier heads that just had no clue about a computer or what it could do," said Jobs. "And so they just grabbed defeat from the greatest victory in the computer industry. Xerox could have owned the entire computer industry today."[18]

When it comes to innovation, Jobs is fond of quoting Picasso's famous dictum: good artists copy, great artists steal. To which Jobs adds: "And we have always been shameless about stealing great ideas."

The Creative Connection

For Jobs, innovation is about creativity, putting things together in unique ways. "Creativity is just connecting things," Jobs told *Wired* magazine. "When you ask creative people how they did something, they feel a little guilty because they didn't really do it, they just saw something. It seemed obvious to them after a while. That's because they were able to connect experiences they've had and synthesize new things. And the reason they were able to do that was that they've had more experiences or they have thought more about their experiences than other people.... Unfortunately, that's too rare a commodity. A lot of people in our industry haven't had very diverse experiences. So they don't have enough dots to connect, and they end up with very linear solutions without a broad perspective on the problem. The broader one's understanding of the human experience, the better design we will have."[19]

Apple's use of magnetism is a good example of how the company takes a technology—something as simple as magnets—and plays with it, putting it to different uses. The first magnets appeared in the latches of Apple's notebooks. A magnet would pull the latch out of its housing as the lid was closed. Then Apple added magnets to its remote controls, so that they could be safely stored attached to the side of the computer. Newer MacBooks have dispensed with latches altogether in favor of stronger magnets that hold their lids closed when not in use; they also have MagSafe power adapters which stay in place thanks to magnets. They are designed to easily detach from the power cord, stopping the computer from crashing to the floor. It's an idea Apple took from Japanese rice cookers, which have had magnetic power adapters for several years for the same reason—to prevent boiling water from being thrown across the kitchen if a child snags the power cord.

Jobs has said that everything he learned about products he

learned from Heathkits as a kid. Heathkits were popular kits for building electronics like ham radios, amplifiers, and oscillators. The kits taught Jobs that products were manifestations of human ingenuity, not magical objects dropped from the sky. "It gave a tremendous level of self-confidence, that through exploration and learning one could understand seemingly very complex things in one's environment," he said. "My childhood was very fortunate in that way."[20]

Jobs has always been a keen student of design, of architecture, and of technology. His offices would be full of electronics devices he'd dismantled to see how they worked. John Sculley remembered that Jobs was always studying other manufacturer's products. "... [E]lectronic parts and cases of products were scattered about the room," he wrote. "It was cluttered and disorganized, with posters and pictures taped to the walls. He had just returned from Japan with a new product that he had taken apart. Pieces of it were on his desk. Whenever Steve saw something new that he was curious about, I discovered, he would buy it, take it apart and try to understand how it worked." [21]

Sculley recalled a trip he and Jobs took to Japan to meet with Akio Morita, the legendary cofounder of Sony. Morita presented the pair with two of the first Walkman players off the production lines. "Steve was fascinated by it," Sculley recalled. "So the first thing he did with his was take it apart and he looked at every single part. How the fit and finish was done. How it was built."[22]

Jobs often took staff on tours of museums and to special

exhibits to educate them about design or architecture. He took the Mac development team to an exhibit by the great Art Nouveau designer Louis Comfort Tiffany, because Tiffany was an artist who commercialized his work. At NeXT, Jobs took a group on a field trip to Frank Lloyd Wright's Fallingwater house in Pennsylvania to study the great architect's design. At NeXT, Jobs would often wander over to the Sony offices across the hall. He'd pick up Sony's brochures, carefully examining the fonts and layouts and the weight of the paper.

On one occasion, Sculley found Jobs madly dashing around the parking lot at Apple's HQ examining cars. He was analyzing the details of their design, looking for cues that he could use in the design of the Macintosh case. "Look at the Mercedes design," he told Sculley, "the proportion of sharp detail to flowing lines. Over the years they've made the design softer but the details starker. That's what we have to do with the Macintosh."[23]

Jobs has had a long-standing interest in German design. In the eighties, his bachelor mansion was empty except for a grand piano and a big black BMW bike. He's always greatly admired Braun, the German electronics manufacturer best known for its clean industrial design. Braun blended high technology with artistic design. Jobs has said several times that he thinks technological creativity and artistic creativity are two sides of the same coin. When asked by *Time* magazine about the difference between art and technology, Jobs said: "I've never believed that they're separate. Leonardo da Vinci was a great artist and a great scientist. Michelangelo knew a tremendous amount about how to cut stone at the quarry. The finest dozen computer scientists I know are all musicians. Some are better than others, but they all consider that an important part of their life. I don't believe that the best people in any of these fields see themselves as one branch of a forked tree. I just don't see that. People bring these things together a lot. Dr. Land at Polaroid said, 'I want Polaroid to stand at the intersection of art and science,' and I've never forgotten that. I think that that's possible, and I think a lot of people have tried."[24]

Flexible Thinking

Apple used to be fiercely proprietary, fielding its own technology and shunning industry standards. During its early years, Apple used nonstandard technology for almost everything. Keyboards, mice, and monitors all used nonstandard connectors. But since Jobs has returned, Apple has become much more flexible and practical. It is shedding a lot of its baggage. Across the board, Apple uses as many standard components and connections as possible, like USB or Intel's chips. The Mac even supports the two-button mouse.

Creativity is being open and flexible, and not protecting your business model. There's got to be an element of reckless abandon, a willingness to bet the company on the next new thing. One example is Jobs's decision to open the iPod to Windows. Initially, the iPod was conceived as Mac-only. Jobs wanted to use it as bait to snare Windows users. He hoped it would be an incentive to switch to the Mac. There was a long, hard debate inside Apple. "There was a long discussion," said Jon Rubinstein, former head of Apple's hardware and iPod divisions. "It was an important decision for us. We didn't know what the effect was going to be, so we debated both sides of the argument, we played devil's advocate."

Rubinstein said they eventually decided that giving Windows users a taste of Apple's technology would have a "halo effect"—it would give a saintly glow to the rest of the company's products. "In the end the halo effect was much more important than losing a few Mac sales," Rubinstein said. "The iPod would get people to go into stores, and they'd check out the Mac at the same time." Rubinstein said the combination of retail stores, the iPod, Macs, and iTunes on Windows was all part and parcel of the same strategy. "They feed off each other," he said. "They use iTunes on Windows and say, 'that's what it's like on the Mac.' "[25]

Jobs introduced the first Windows-compatible iPod in July 2002. The iPod was formatted for Windows but it still needed a FireWire connection, which was rare on Windows computers. The real change occurred nearly a year later, when Apple enhanced the way the iPod connects to a Windows computer. In May 2003, with the introduction of the third-generation iPod, Apple added USB 2 connectivity instead of just the standard FireWire. Adding USB 2 was a hugely important shift for Steve Jobs. It marked a departure from his principle of making products primarily for the Mac platform. But it also had the most dramatic impact on sales. Prior to the May 2003 switch, Apple had sold one million iPods. But within the next six months, it sold another million iPods, and nearly three million more were sold within a year. In the next eighteen months, nine million more were sold. The iPod is now firmly a Windows device. All iPods are formatted for Windows—not the Mac—out of the box. But whereas Windows computers aren't compatible with Mac file formats, the Mac is, and they have no trouble connecting to Windows-formatted iPods.

Likewise, other Apple devices are Windows-friendly. In 2007, Apple released its Safari browser for Windows: another attempt to create a halo effect around its software, especially as a lot of Windows users are using Safari on their iPhones. The iPhone works as well with Windows and Microsoft Outlook as it does on a Mac. AppleTV is Windows compatible, as are Apple's Airport WiFi base stations. Apple's old modus operandi of keeping its technology proprietary has been thrown out of the window. Jobs has fully embraced the world of Windows.

Sir Howard Stringer is trying hard to reinvigorate Sony, to bring back some of the vigorous inventiveness that built and defined the company, but the company seems to have lost its flair for innovation. Digital music is the perfect example. This is a business Sony should have owned. Sony invented portable music with the Walkman and continued to dominate the portable device market even after dozens of other companies turned out Walkman and Discman knockoffs. But in trying to protect its music labels, Sony crippled its early digital players. Amazingly, Sony's digital Walkman couldn't play MP3 files, even though that was the emerging standard for digital music. Instead, Sony forced users to convert their music to Sony's proprietary ATRAC format, which understandably they were loathe to do. They already had reams of music in MP3 format on their computers, which couldn't be played on Sony's players.

Jobs's willingness to try open-ended experiments and then refine the ideas isn't seen at many other companies. At Sony, for example, managers often show up to meetings with a single screenshot and say, "This is our design." One engineer, who's worked closely with the Japanese giant for several years, said he saw this many times. Puzzled and slightly shocked, he'd ask how they arrived at that particular design: What were the choices they made? Why did they do it this way instead of that? But his questions would always be rebuffed with a curt "This is the approved design."

"They think they are really innovative, but they're scared to do anything new," the engineer explained. "A huge part of it is getting the blame. They're so terrified of making a mistake, they always go with what they've done before."[26]

The same is true when it comes to hardware. When developing a product, Sony managers would often present a list of the features in competing products and use that as the blueprint. But by the time the Sony product came out, the market had moved on. Rubinstein told me that the iPod should have been Sony's product. "The Sony Walkman changed how people listened to music," he said. "How they [let that] slip through their fingers I'll never understand. They should have owned it. The iPod should have been Sony." Rubinstein said Sony didn't develop the iPod because it was afraid of hurting its other products. "A lot of it is fear of killing your own products," he said. "You don't want to kill your products if they're successful."[27] But Jobs isn't afraid. He killed Apple's most popular iPod model—the mini—at the height of its popularity in favor of a newer, thinner model, the nano. "Steve drives a lot of that," said Rubinstein. "He's a burn-the-boats kind of guy. If you burn the boats, you have to stand and fight."[28]

Apple's phenomenally successful retail stores are an unlikely but telling example of Apple's innovation at work. The stores were born of necessity, inspired by the digital hub, and developed like all of Apple's products—prototyped, tested, and refined.

An Apple Innovation Case Study: The Retail Stores

Drive to your local upscale mall and chances are you'll find an Apple Store. Nestled among the frilly Lane Bryants and Victoria's Secrets, you'll see a high-tech boutique full of shiny white plastic and silver metal. The store has no name—just a big, brightly lit Apple logo in the middle of a stainless steel facade. Below the store's metal forehead, you'll see a big wide-open window with an eye-catching display showcasing the latest iPhones or iPods.

Step inside and you'll find the store is a modest size, not too big and not too small. It will be packed with people; they always are. There's often a line to get in when the store opens, and there are a few stragglers reluctant to leave when it closes at night.

The store is very seductive. You feel like you're in a vision of a Kubrickian future—full of gleaming space-age hardware. It is inviting and low key. You're free to play around with everything on display, and you can hang around as long as you want. You answer some e-mail and play a couple of games. There's no pressure to spend any money, and the staff is happy to answer any question, even the most basic. Later on in the evening there's a class on video editing at a small theater at the back of the store. The class is free.

Apple opened its first retail store on May 19, 2001, in Glendale, California, and since then its chain of more than two hundred stores has become the hottest thing in retail.

Apple's chain of stores is the fastest growing in retail history, reaching $1 billion in annual sales in just three years, besting the record previously held by The Gap. By spring 2006, the stores were making $1 billion every quarter.

The stores account for a big—and growing—chunk of Apple's business, and are playing a key role in the company's comeback. The growth of the stores coincided with the huge growth of the iPod. Customers went to the stores to check out the iPod, but stayed to play with the Macs—and sales of both took off.

The stores are insanely profitable. One Apple store can make as much money as six other stores in the same mall combined—and can pull in almost the same revenue as a big Best Buy store, but with only 10 percent of the floor space.

The stores are like high-end clothes boutiques. They are swish and stylish, selling a lifestyle, not a cheapo box. There is no pressure to spend, and the staff is friendly and helpful. The service makes all the difference. Apple's stores are no-pressure hangouts where customers can play with the machines and leave without guilt, very unlike the cacophony and harsh lighting at the big box retailers. There are no aggressive salespeople ready to pounce and pressure customers into purchasing expensive accessories and unnecessary extended warranties.

This is basic stuff for some, but for a huge swath of the population, some friendly, simple guidance is key to making a sale. It's amazing how important this is for gaining new customers who are unfamiliar with the technology. I recently overheard one potential customer asking if he needed a computer to use his new iPod. Another booked a session at the Genius Bar, which is normally reserved for troubleshooting, to learn how to plug her iPod into her computer and transfer music.

When a customer buys a new Mac, the machine is personalized for them, for free, before they leave the store. Staff will load up drivers for the customer's printer or camera, and help set up an Internet connection. Switchers from Windows love this kind of hand-holding, and it's vastly different from shopping at big box stores where the only contact is the security guard checking your bag or cart as you leave.

The stores are extremely busy. They are always full and often packed. According to Apple, they are some of the busiest retail stores in the industry, rivaling big grocery stores and popular restaurants. When Apple opens a new store, there's always a line of fans who camp out the night before. Some fans travel to every opening in their area, and a dedicated few fly international or cross-country to big store openings in London, Tokyo, or California.

When Jobs returned to Apple, he knew that the company needed a retail presence just to survive. Before Apple launched its stores, its only direct contact with customers was at the Macworld conferences, which attracted at their height about 80,000 conference attendees to a pair of biannual meets. (These days, more than 80,000 people visit Apple's stores every morning, and another 80,000 in the afternoon!)

In the mid-1990s, Macs were sold through mail order catalogs or at retailers like Circuit City or Sears, where they were often relegated to a dusty back shelf. Neglected and ignored, the Macs got scant attention. Sales reps steered customers to the Windows PCs up front. Things were so bad for Apple that some Mac fans took it upon themselves to staff the stores on nights and weekends as unofficial salespeople, trying desperately to sell Macs in their spare time.

In the late 1990s, Apple started experimenting with mini

stores-within-stores at CompUSA, which was a minor success, telling Jobs that Apple needed to expand its high-street presence, while making shopping for a Mac a more Apple-like experience. But Jobs wanted total control, which he could achieve only if Apple opened its own stores. Jobs wanted "the best buying experience for its products, and thought that most of the resellers weren't investing enough in their stores or making other selling improvements," Jobs told the *Wall Street Journal*. Note Jobs's telling phrase: "the best buying experience." Like all of Jobs's endeavors the stores are driven by the customers' experience.

At the time, Jobs said 95 percent of consumers "don't even consider Apple," and the company needed a place with knowledgeable staff to show how the Mac could become the center of their lives. The stores would especially target Windows users. It would be a friendly place for them to check out Macs. An early tag line for the stores said, "5 down, 95 to go," referring to the 5 percent Mac market share compared to Microsoft's 95 percent.

Jobs was wary of getting burned in retail, so he did his usual trick of recruiting the best person he could find, who turned out to be Millard "Mickey" Drexler, president and CEO of The Gap. In May 1999, Drexler joined Apple's board. Drexler's "expertise in marketing and retail will be a tremendous resource as Apple continues to grow in the consumer market," said Jobs in a press release. "He will add a completely new dimension to Apple's board."

Jobs then called Ron Johnson, a retail veteran who'd helped

turn Target from a Wal-Mart also-ran into an up-market pur-
veyor of affordable design. Johnson had recruited name-brand
designers to design housewares for Target, which earned it the
French-sounding nickname Tar-jay. "Eight years later, design is
the cornerstone of their business strategy," said Johnson, now
Apple's senior vice president for retail.[29]

Jobs hired Johnson, a big, friendly Midwesterner with floppy
gray hair and a wide smile, in January 2000. His first three
words to him were "Retailing is hard." Jobs added, "We're going to operate with a little bit of fear, because retailing is a hard
business."[30]

At first Johnson couldn't tell anyone he was working for
Apple. He used the alias John Bruce (a variation on his middle
name) and a phony title to stop competitors from getting wind
of Apple's retail plans. Johnson didn't start using his real name,
even inside the company, until after Apple had opened several
stores.

When Apple opened its first retail store in May 2001, most
pundits thought the company was making a costly mistake.
Gateway, the only other computer company with its own retail
stores, was closing them down. Gateway's stores weren't attracting customers. Inexplicably, Gateway's stores didn't carry
any inventory. Customers could check out the goods, but had
to order them online, which killed the opportunity to make im-
pulse sales. Instead, Gateway's customers gravitated to the big
box stores where they could compare offerings from different
manufacturers—and buy what they wanted there and then.

Meanwhile, Apple hadn't yet shown much sign of a turn-around. The Internet bubble was bursting, the NASDAQ was in the tank, and Dell, which seemed to have the perfect business model for computers—sell direct over the Internet—was crushing all comers. Apple's revenues had shrunk from $12 billion to $5 billion, and it was only just posting a profit. The iPod wouldn't be launched for another six months (and when it did, no one had any idea of the smash hit it would become). It seemed like the worst possible time for a struggling company to embark on an expensive, unproven experiment in retail.

"I give them two years before they're turning out the lights on a very painful and expensive mistake," retail expert David A. Goldstein told *Business Week*, echoing a sentiment widely held at the time. Not one industry watcher, Wall Street analyst, or journalist went on record to say it was a good idea. "Few outsiders think new stores, no matter how well-conceived, will get Apple back on the hot-growth path," *Business Week* said.[31]

Enriching Lives Along the Way

Until the 1990s, most stores sold goods from a variety of manufacturers, the department store model. But in the late 1980s, The Gap revolutionized retail by dropping other brands and concentrating on its own line of clothing. Peddling mountains of stylish but affordable "casual basics," The Gap took off like a rocket. It went from $480 million in revenues in 1983 to $13.7 billion in 2000 and entered the history books as the fastest growing retail chain. (It went sideways after that, but that's a different story.) Now The Gap's model has been emulated by dozens of retailers, especially in apparel, but also by tech firms like Sony, Nokia, and Samsung. Even Dell, the perennial web-only retailer in the boom years of the nineties, is opening booths at malls and selling computers through Wal-Mart, Costco, and the French Carrefour supermarket chain in Europe.

Most retailers are interested only in selling as much merchandise as possible. Gateway called it "moving metal." This philosophy led Gateway to certain inevitable conclusions: be low cost, compete on price, and put stores where real estate is cheap, like out-of-the-way parking lots. But all these decisions turned out to be disastrous.

The biggest problem: no one visited Gateway's stores. Most people buy a new computer every two or three years. To shop at a Gateway store, customers had to go out of their way. The store wasn't located where they did their shopping—in the mall. The store was in a remote parking lot. At the height of Gateway's retail operation, when the company owned nearly 200 stores employing about 2,500 people, traffic was 250 people a week. That's right: 250 visitors *a week*. In April 2004, after several years of spotty sales, Gateway shuttered all its stores—a very painful and expensive mistake.

On the other hand, Jobs wanted to bring customers into the store. He wanted a "lifestyle" store where customers could get a taste of the Apple digital lifestyle—and hopefully leave with a machine.

One of the key early decisions was to locate the stores in high-traffic areas. This first decision proved to be the breakthrough but was initially universally criticized, because popular locations would be expensive.

Apple chose high-end malls and trendy shopping districts, not low-rent strip malls on the edge of town. The idea was to get foot traffic, to build the kind of store where the curious could drop in and learn what it's like on the other side, the Mac side. If most computer shoppers didn't even consider Apple when buying a new computer, they certainly weren't going to drive twenty minutes to a remote store in a remote parking lot. "The real estate was a lot more expensive," Jobs told *Fortune*. But people "didn't have to gamble with 20 minutes of their time. They only had to gamble with 20 footsteps of their time."[32] It's the old real-estate mantra—location, location, location.

Apple planned the locations very carefully using census data and information about its registered customers. Apple has never revealed the criteria it uses for choosing store locations, but Gary Allen, a close watcher of Apple's retail strategy who runs ifoAppleStore.com., a website devoted to the chain, has pieced together some of the company's process. According to Allen, it's a combination of the number of registered Apple customers in the area, certain demographics, particularly age and average household income, and proximity to major schools and universities, and—cleverly—major interstate highways.

The biggest problem Apple faced was finding a space in suitable malls. Apple waited three years for a good location in San Francisco, the company's hometown.

In an early strategy meeting with Jobs, Ron Johnson was presented with Apple's entire product line: two portable computers and two desktop computers. This was before the launch of the iPod. Johnson was faced with the prospect of filling 6,000-square-foot stores with just four products. "And that was a challenge," Johnson recalled. "But it ended up being the ultimate opportunity, because we said, 'because we don't have enough products to fill a store that size, let's fill it with the ownership experience.' "[33]

When Jobs and Johnson started thinking about the stores, they started with an unusual vision—to "enrich lives," Johnson said. "When we envisioned Apple's retail model, we said it's got to connect with Apple. Very easy... enrich lives. Enriching lives. That's what Apple has been doing for 30-plus years."[34]

The goal to enrich lives led to two clear objectives: to design the stores around the customer experience, and to be aware of the ownership experience for the lifetime of the product.

First, designing the store around the customer experience is not the same as designing around the retail experience. Most retailers concentrate on how customers find and select items in the store, and then get them to spend as much as possible. But Jobs and Johnson asked themselves how the products would fit into the context of customers' lives, their life experience.

Johnson explained: "We didn't think about their experience in the store. We said, 'let's design this store around their life experience.'"

Second, "We said, we want our stores to create an ownership experience for the customer," explained Johnson. The store should be about the lifetime of the product, not the moment of the transaction. At many stores, the purchase ends the relationship with the store. At Apple stores, "We like to think that's where it begins."

"So first we made a list," Johnson said. "Enrich lives—how do you do it?" They decided the store should carry only the right stuff. Too much merchandise confuses customers. Johnson learned the benefits of limiting choice at Target. Some of Target's executives wanted to stock the shelves with as many products as possible. At one time, Target carried thirty-one toaster models. But Johnson learned that the leading retailer in kitchen supply—Williams Sonoma—stocked only two toasters. "It's not about broad assortment," he said. "It's about the right assortment." [35]

Jobs and Johnson also decided customers should be encouraged to test-drive all the products. At the time, most computer stores had working models on display, but customers couldn't load up software or connect to the Net or download pictures from their digital camera. At the Apple stores, customers would be free to test all aspects of a machine before they bought it.

At first, Jobs pondered the idea of opening a few stores and seeing what happened. But on Mickey Drexler's advice, Jobs had a secret mockup store built in a warehouse close to Apple's Cupertino HQ. The store would be designed the same way as Apple's products: they would build a prototype that could be refined and improved until it was perfected.

Johnson assembled a team of about twenty retail experts and store designers, and began to experiment with different store layouts. To make it friendly and approachable, the team decided to use natural materials: wood, stone, glass, and stainless steel. The palette was neutral and the stores would have very good lighting to make the products glow. Typically, there was an uncompromising attention to detail. In the early days, Jobs met with the design team for half a day each week. During one meeting, the group exhaustively evaluated three types of lighting just to make sure multicolored iMacs would shine as they do in glossy print ads, according to *Business 2.0* magazine. "Every little element in the store is designed to these very details," Johnson said.[36]

In October 2000, after several months of work, the prototype store was nearly ready when Johnson had a revelation. He realized that the store didn't reflect Apple's digital hub philosophy, which put the computer at the heart of the digital lifestyle. The prototype store was laid out with computers in one corner and cameras in another, just like at Best Buy. Johnson realized that the store should group the computers with the cameras to show customers how they could use the Mac to actually do things, like assemble a book of digital photographs or burn a home movie to DVD.

"Steve, I think it's wrong," Johnson told Jobs. "I think we're making a mistake. This is about digital future, not just about products."[37] Johnson realized that it would be more effective to show customers functioning digital hubs, with cameras, camcorders, and MP3 players attached to computers. The working machines would be arranged in "solution zones," showing how the Mac could be used for digital photography, video editing, and making music—activities prospective customers would actually want to do.

At first, Jobs was far from happy: "Do you know what you're saying? Do you know we have to start over?" Jobs yelled, angrily storming off to his office. But Jobs soon had a change of heart. Within the hour, Jobs returned to Johnson's office in a brighter mood. He told Johnson that almost all of Apple's best products had been shelved and started over, like the iMac. It was part of the process. In a later interview with *Fortune*, Jobs said his initial reaction was "Oh, God, we're screwed!" but Johnson was right. "It cost us, I don't know, six, nine months. But it was the right decision by a million miles," he said.[38]

After the redesign, the prototype store was divided into four sections, each devoted to Johnson's "solution zones." One quarter at the front of the store is devoted to products, another quarter to music and photos, the third quarter to the Genius Bar and movies, and the fourth quarter to accessories and other products at the back of the store. The idea is to create a place where customers could find entire "solutions" to lifestyle problems they wanted solved—like taking and sharing digital pictures or editing and making DVDs.

The stores are designed to be a public place, like a library, and more than just a place to display products. "We don't want the store to be about the product, but about a series of experiences that make it more than a store," Johnson said.[39]

Apple makes sure the stores are always packed by giving unlimited access to Internet computers and arranging lots of in-store events. Every week, there are free workshops, classes, and—at the bigger stores—talks by creative professionals and performances by bands. During the summer, Apple Camp attracts thousands of school kids to take computer lessons during the traditionally quiet summer months.

The bigger flagship stores would have staircases made of glass, simply to encourage customers to climb to the second floor, which is traditionally lightly trafficked. (The glass staircases became major attractions and won several awards.)

Cozying on Up to the Genius Bar

The most important innovation has been offering hands-on training and support at the Genius Bar. In 2000, computer repairs could take several weeks. Customers had to phone tech support, ship the machine to the company, and wait for it to be returned. "That's not enriching someone's life," Johnson said.[40]

Apple decided it would offer turnaround on repairs in days, rivaling service at the neighborhood dry cleaner.

The Genius Bar has become the most distinctive feature of Apple's stores, and the most popular. Customers love that they're able to troubleshoot problems face to face, or drop off malfunctioning equipment at the local mall rather than send it in. "Customers love our Genius Bars," Johnson said.

Apple estimated that in 2006, more than one million people visited the Genius Bars during an average week. At the flagship stores, there are often lines of people waiting for the Genius Bar before the store has opened. They are almost too successful. Thanks to the phenomenal growth in visitors to the stores, the Genius Bars are becoming oversubscribed, and many have implemented appointment schedules to cope with the demand.

The idea of a Genius Bar came from customers. Johnson asked a focus group what was their best experience with customer service, anywhere. Most mentioned the concierge desk at hotels, which is there to help, not sell. Johnson realized it might be a good idea to install a concierge desk for computers. He thought it could be like a friendly neighborhood bar, where the bartender dispensed free advice instead of booze.

When Johnson first suggested the idea to Jobs, his boss was skeptical. Jobs liked the idea of face-to-face support, but having known a lot of geeks, Jobs was afraid they wouldn't have the people skills to deal with the public. But Johnson persuaded him that most young people are very familiar with computers and they would have little trouble hiring personable, service-oriented staffers who were proficient with technology.

The most significant idea Johnson had about staffing was to dispense with sales commissions, which are pretty standard in consumer electronics retailing. "People thought I was crazy at Apple," he said.[41] But Johnson didn't want the stores to become sales-driven pressure cookers. He wanted the staff in the customers' hearts, not their wallets.

Apple staffers must gently persuade customers—many of them Windows users who are skeptical about Apple—to switch to the Mac. Johnson knew that for most potential customers, this wasn't going to be a snap decision. They were likely to visit the store three or four times before taking the plunge, and the last thing Johnson wanted was customers worrying that the guy they started with wasn't on duty.

Instead of paying commissions, Johnson decided to enhance their status. The best staff would graduate to a Mac Genius or a presenter in the theater. "Your job is elevated to positions of status such as I'm a Mac Genius. I'm the smartest Mac person in town. People request me on the Internet, to come meet me at the store so I can help them," Johnson said. "My job is to make the store rich with experience for people."

The lack of a commission elevates the job from a purely mercantile position, and makes it much more like a profession. Even though many of the staff work part-time, or are paid by the hour, they enjoy some of the status of a professional. Johnson says, "It's not the boring, laborious I've-got-to-move-merchandise-and-take-care-of-customer problems. I'm suddenly enriching people's lives. And that's how we select, that's how we motivate, that's how we train our people." This is classic Apple, of course: even retail has been instilled with a sense of mission.

Apple tries to recruit creative computerphiles fresh out of school, the kind of kids who think working at the Apple store would be a good first job. As an incentive, Apple offers in-house training. While working at the store, staff members are taught how to use professional software applications like Final Cut Pro, Garageband, and other applications that may prove useful later on. The turnover rate is relatively low for retail: about 20 percent, when the industry average is above 50 percent, according to Apple.

The stores are evolving from well-designed shopping centers into learning environments. Apple has been adding additional advice "bars" at some of the bigger stores, including an iPod bar for advice and repair, and a Studio bar to help customers with creative projects, like making movies or laying out photo books. The idea of free advice bars is beginning to spread to other retailers. Whole Foods grocery, for example, in 2006 started experimenting with an advice bar for recipes and ingredients at a store in Austin, Texas.

When most computer companies sell their wares at high-volume big box stores, and offer support only by phone, Apple's stores are a radically different proposition. Johnson calls the stores "high touch," a phrase that means dealing with a human instead of a computer. The term is sometimes used to mean good customer service. Nordstrom and Starbucks are said to be high touch, but no one had tried it with computers. "In a high-tech world, wouldn't it be nice to have some high touch?" Johnson said. Jobs and Johnson decided to put good service into computer shopping and change the way people shopped for technology.

The retail stores demonstrate Apple's innovation at work. The philosophy, design, and layout came from the digital hub strategy, and the execution from Jobs's uncompromising focus on the customer experience.

Lessons from Steve

- *Don't lose sight of the customer.* The Cube bombed because it was built for designers, not customers.
- *Study the market and the industry.* Jobs is constantly looking to see what new technologies are coming down the pike.
- *Don't consciously think about innovation.* Systemizing innovation is like watching Michael Dell try to dance. *Painful.*
- *Concentrate on products.* Products are the gravitational force that pulls it all together.
- *Remember that motives make a difference.* Concentrate on great products, not becoming the biggest or the richest.
- *Steal.* Be shameless about stealing other people's great ideas.
- *Connect.* For Jobs, creativity is simply connecting things.
- *Study.* Jobs is a keen student of art, design, and architecture. He evens runs around parking lots looking at Mercedeses.
- *Be flexible.* Jobs dropped a lot of long-cherished traditions that made Apple special—and kept it small.
- *Burn the boats.* Jobs killed the most popular iPod to make room for a new, thinner model. Burn the boats, and you must stand and fight.
- *Prototype.* Even Apple's stores were developed like every other product: protoyped, edited, and refined.
- *Ask customers.* The popular Genius Bar came from customers.

Chapter 7

Case Study: How It All Came Together with the iPod

"Software is the user experience. As the iPod and iTunes prove, it has become the driving technology not just of computers but of consumer electronics."

—Steve Jobs

T he iPod is the product that transformed Apple from a struggling PC company into an electronics powerhouse. How the iPod came together illustrates a lot of the points discussed in previous chapters: It was the product of small teams working closely together. It was born of Jobs's innovation strategy: the digital hub. Its design was guided by an understanding of the customer experience—how to navigate a big library of digital tunes. It came together through Apple's iterative design process, and some of the key ideas came from unlikely sources (the scroll wheel was suggested by an advertising executive, not a designer). Many of the key components were sourced from outside the company, but Apple combined them in a unique, innovative way. And it was designed in such secrecy that not even Jobs knew that Apple had already trademarked the iPod name.

But most of all, the iPod was truly a team effort. "We had a lot of brainstorming sessions," explained one insider. "Products at Apple happen very organically. There [are] lots of meetings, with lots of people, lots of ideas. It's a team approach."[1]

Revisiting the Digital Hub

Necessity is the mother of invention. Apple started writing application software for OS X because other companies balked, and it's turned out to be another golden opportunity for the company.

In 2000, the iMac was leading the charge for Apple's comeback, but Jobs's attempts to persuade developers to write software for OS X was getting a mixed reception.

Jobs's deal with Bill Gates ensured that Microsoft would produce new versions of Office and its Internet Explorer browser for OS X. But Adobe, one of the biggest software makers for the Mac, had flatly refused to adopt its consumer-level software for OS X.

"They said flat-out no," Jobs told *Fortune* magazine. "We were shocked, because they had been a big supporter in the early days of the Mac. But we said, 'Okay, if nobody wants to help us, we're just going to have to do this ourselves.'"

At the same time, consumers were beginning to buy lots of devices designed to be plugged into computers—Palm Pilots, digital cameras, and camcorders—but in Jobs's view, there was no good software to manage pictures or edit home movies on either the Mac or Windows.

Jobs figured that if Apple could build software to enhance these devices—to make editing a home movie easy, for instance—customers might buy Macs to manage their pictures, edit video, and synchronize their cell phones. The Mac would become the digital hub of the home, the technology centerpiece to connect all these digital devices.

As described in Chapter 6, Jobs spelled out the PC's third great age at the 2001 Macworld. "This age is spawned by the proliferation of digital devices everywhere: CD players, MP3 players, cell phones, handheld organizers, digital cameras, digital camcorders, and more. We're confident that the Mac can be the hub of this new digital lifestyle by adding value to these other devices."[2]

The digital hub is a fresh spin on the old "killer apps" strategy that has long driven the technology business. Customers rarely buy computers for the hardware alone; they're more interested in the software it can run. An exclusive piece of killer software is usually enough to guarantee the success of the machine it runs on. The Apple II was a hit thanks to VisiCalc, the first spreadsheet. Nintendo became a force in the console business thanks to its Mario Brothers games. And the Mac took off only after Adobe developed PostScript, a standard language for documents and printers, which launched the desktop publishing revolution.

Jobs's digital hub strategy has been a mixed success. The software it inspired—applications like iPhoto, iMovie, and Garageband—have been highly praised by critics, and are regarded by some as the best on any platform. But, on their own, they have failed to attract new users to the Mac in huge numbers. They haven't proven to be killer apps.

Nonetheless, as corporate strategy, the idea of the computer as a digital hub has been phenomenally successful, and still is.

When most observers were still comparing Apple to Microsoft and couldn't see beyond the old battle for the enterprise, Jobs focused on consumers and saw the looming digital entertainment revolution. Computers were becoming the key *lifestyle* technology, not just the key *work* technology. From the digital hub idea rose Apple's suite of software apps, which are becoming the lifestyle equivalent of Microsoft's Office suite. And, as we've seen, it also inspired the iPod, the iTunes music store, and Apple's phenomenally successful retail stores.

Jobs's Misstep: Customers Wanted Music, Not Video

One of the primary features of the early iMac was its ability to connect to consumer camcorders via a FireWire port. FireWire is standard equipment on many consumer camcorders, and the iMac was one of the first consumer computers designed as a home-video-editing station.

Jobs had long been interested in video, and thought that the iMac had the potential to do for video what the first Mac had done for desktop publishing. The first piece of digital hub software Jobs created was iMovie, an easy-to-use video-editing application.

Trouble is, in the late 1990s, consumers were more interested in digital music than digital video. Jobs was so consumed by video, he didn't notice the beginnings of the digital music revolution. Jobs has a reputation as a technology seer. Supposedly, he has the ability to divine future technology—the graphical user interface, the mouse, stylish MP3 players—but he totally missed the millions of music lovers who were trading tunes by the billions on Napster and other file-sharing networks. Users were ripping their CD collections and sharing tunes over the Internet. In 2000, music started migrating from the stereo to the computer. The rush to digital was especially marked in dorm rooms and, though college kids were a big source of iMac sales, Apple had no jukebox software for managing collections of digital music.

In January 2001, Apple announced a loss of $195 million thanks to a general economic downturn and a sharp decline in sales. It was the first and only quarterly loss since Jobs returned. Customers had stopped buying iMacs without CD burners. In a conference call with analysts, Jobs admitted that

Apple had "missed the boat" by excluding recordable CD burners from the iMac line.[3] He was chastened. "I felt like a dope," Jobs said later. "I thought we had missed it. We had to work hard to catch up."[4]

Other PC makers hadn't missed it, though. Hewlett-Packard, for one, was shipping CD burners with its computers, a major feature that Apple had to follow. To catch up, Apple licensed a popular music player called SoundJam MP from a small company and hired its hotshot programmer, Jeff Robbin. Under the direction of Jobs, Robbin spent several months retooling SoundJam into iTunes (mostly making it simpler). Jobs introduced it at the Macworld Expo show in January 2001.

"Apple has done what Apple does best: make complex applications easy, and make them even more powerful in the process," Jobs told the keynote crowd. "And we hope its dramatically simpler user interface will bring even more people into the digital music revolution."

While Robbin was working on iTunes, Jobs and his executive team started looking at gadgets to see if there were any opportunities. They found that digital cameras and camcorders were pretty well designed, but music players were a different matter. "The products stank," Greg Joswiak, vice president of iPod product marketing, told *Newsweek*.[5]

Digital music players were either big and clunky or small and useless. Most were based on fairly small memory chips, either 32 or 64 Mbytes in size, which allowed them to store only a few dozen songs—not much better than a cheap portable CD player.

But a couple of the players were based on a new 2.5-inch hard drive from Fujitsu. The most popular was the Nomad Jukebox from Singapore-based Creative. About the size of a portable CD player but twice as heavy, the Nomad Jukebox showed the promise of storing thousands of songs on a (smallish) device. But it had some horrible flaws: It used USB 1 to transfer songs manually from the computer, which was painfully slow. The interface was an engineer special (unbelievably awful). And it often sucked batteries dry in just forty-five minutes.

Here was Apple's opportunity.

"I don't know whose idea it was to do a music player, but Steve jumped on it pretty quick and he asked me to look into it," said Jon Rubinstein, a veteran engineer who headed up Apple's hardware division for more than a decade.[6] Now the executive chairman of the board at Palm, Rubinstein is a tall, thin New Yorker in his early fifties with a frank, no-bullshit manner and an easy smile.

He joined Apple in 1997 from NeXT, where he'd been Jobs's hardware guy. While at Apple, Rubinstein oversaw a string of groundbreaking machines, from the first Bondi-blue iMac to water-cooled workstations and, of course, the iPod. When Apple split into separate iPod and Macintosh divisions in 2004, Rubinstein was put in charge of the iPod side, a testament to how important both he and the iPod were to Apple.

Apple's team knew it could solve most of the problems

that plagued the Nomad. Its FireWire connector could quickly transfer songs from computer to player: an entire CD in a few seconds, a huge library of MP3s in minutes. And thanks to the rapidly growing cell phone industry, new batteries and displays were constantly coming to market. This is Jobs's "vectors in time"—keeping an eye out for advantageous technological advances. Future versions of the iPod could take advantage of improvements in cell phone technology.

In February 2001, during the annual Macworld Expo in Tokyo, Rubinstein made a routine visit to Toshiba, Apple's supplier of hard drives, where executives showed him a tiny new drive they'd just developed. The drive was just 1.8 inches in diameter—considerably smaller than the 2.5-inch Fujitsu drive used in competing players—but Toshiba didn't have any ideas what it might be used for. "They said they didn't know what to do with it. Maybe put it in a small notebook," Rubinstein recalled. "I went back to Steve and I said, 'I know how to do this. I've got all the parts.' He said, 'Go for it.'"

"Jon's very good at seeing a technology and very quickly assessing how good it is," Joswiak told *Cornell Engineering Magazine*. "The iPod's a great example of Jon seeing a piece of technology's potential: that very, very small form-factor hard drive."

Rubinstein didn't want to distract any of the engineers working on new Macs, so in February 2001 he hired a consultant, engineer Tony Fadell, to hash out the details. Fadell had a lot of experience making handheld devices: he'd developed popular gadgets for both General Magic and Philips. A mutual acquaintance gave his phone number to Rubinstein. "I called Tony," Rubinstein said. "He was on the ski slope at the time. Until he walked in the door, he didn't know what he was going to be working on."

Jobs wanted a player in stores by the fall, before the holiday shopping season. Fadell was put in charge of a small team of engineers and designers, who put the device together quickly. The iPod was built under a shroud of intense secrecy, Rubinstein said. From beginning to end, among the seven thousand staff that worked at Apple HQ at the time, only fifty to one hundred even knew of the existence of the iPod project. To complete the project as quickly as possible, the team took as many parts as possible off-the-shelf: the drive from Toshiba, a battery from Sony, some control chips from Texas Instruments.

The basic hardware blueprint was bought from a Silicon Valley startup called PortalPlayer, which was working on so-called reference designs for several different digital players, including a full-sized unit for the living room and a portable player about the size of a pack of cigarettes.

The team also drew heavily on Apple's in-house expertise. "We didn't start from scratch," said Rubinstein. "We've got a hardware engineering group at our disposal. We need a power supply, we've got a power supply group. We need a display, we've got a display group. We used the architecture team. This was a highly leveraged product from the technologies we already had in place."

The thorniest problem was battery life. If the drive was kept spinning while playing songs, it quickly drained the batteries. The solution was to load several songs into a bank of memory chips, which draw much less power. The drive could be put to sleep until it was called on to load more songs. While other manufacturers used a similar architecture for skip protection, the first iPod had a 32-Mbyte memory buffer, which allowed batteries to stretch ten hours instead of two or three.

Given the device's parts, the iPod's final shape was obvious. All the pieces sandwiched naturally together into a thin box about the size of a pack of cards.

"Sometimes things are really clear from the materials they are made from, and this was one of those times," said Rubinstein. "It was obvious how it was going to look when it was put together."

Nonetheless, Apple's design group, headed by Jonathan Ive, made prototype after prototype. Ive's design group collaborated closely with manufacturers and engineers, constantly tweaking and refining the design.

To make them easy to debug, the early iPod prototypes were built inside big polycarbonate containers about the size of a big shoebox, known as "stealth units." Like a lot of Silicon Valley companies, Apple is subject to industrial espionage from rivals who would love to get a peek at what it's working on.

Some observers have suggested that the polycarbonate boxes disguised the prototypes from would-be spies. But engineers say the boxes are purely functional: they're big and accessible, and easy to debug if there's a problem.

To save time developing the iPod's software, a basic low-level operating system was also brought in to provide a foundation on which to build. The software was licensed from Pixo, a Silicon Valley startup founded by Paul Mercer, a former Apple engineer who'd worked on the Newton, that was developing an operating system for cell phones. The Pixo system was very low level: it handled things like calls to the hard drive for music files. It also contained libraries for building interfaces, with commands for drawing lines or boxes on a screen. It didn't include a finished user interface. Apple built the iPod's celebrated user interface on top of Pixo's low-level system.

The idea for the scroll wheel was suggested by Apple's head of marketing, Phil Schiller, who in an early meeting said quite definitively, "The wheel is the right user interface for this product." Schiller also suggested that menus should scroll faster the longer the wheel is turned, a stroke of genius that distinguishes the iPod from the agony of using competing players. The idea for the scroll wheel might not have been suggested had Apple followed the traditional serial design process.

The iPod's scroll wheel was its most distinguishing feature. Using a wheel to control an MP3 player was, at the time, unprecedented, but it was surprisingly functional. Competing MP3 players used standard buttons. The scroll wheel appears to have been an act of magical creation. Why hadn't anyone come up with a control device like this before? Schiller's scroll wheel didn't come out of the blue, however; scroll wheels are pretty common in electronics, from mice with scroll wheels to the thumb wheels on the side of some Palm Pilots. Bang & Olufsen BeoCom phones have a very familiar iPod-like dial for navigating lists of phone contacts and calls. Back in 1983, the Hewlett-Packard 9836 workstation had a keyboard with a similar wheel for scrolling text.

On the software side, Jobs charged programmer Jeff Robbin with overseeing the iPod's interface and interaction with iTunes. The interface was mocked up by designer Tim Wasko, the interactive designer who had previously been responsible for the clean, simple interface in Apple's QuickTime player. Like the hardware designers, Wasko designed mockup after mockup, presenting the variations on large glossy printouts that could be spread over a conference table to be quickly sorted and discussed.

"I remember sitting with Steve and some other people night after night from nine until one, working out the user interface for the first iPod," said Robbin. "It evolved by trial and error into something a little simpler every day. We knew we had reached the end when we looked at each other and said, 'Well, of course. Why would we want to do it any other way?' "[7] Like Jonny Ive's hardware prototypes, the iPod's intuitive interface was arrived at through an iterative trial-and-error design process.

Jobs insisted that the iPod work seamlessly with iTunes, and that many functions should be automated, especially transferring songs. The model was the Palm's HotSync software, which automatically updates the Palm Pilots when they're hooked up. Users should be able to plug their iPod into the computer and have songs load automatically onto the player—no user intervention required. This ease of use is one of the great unheralded secrets of the iPod's success. Unlike players before it, the iPod and iTunes alleviated the pain of managing a digital music collection. Most competing players made the user do a lot of work. To load songs, they had to manually drag tunes onto an icon of their MP3 player. It was a pain in the rear, and not something most people wanted to do with their time. The iPod changed that. Here's how Jobs summed up the iPod's easy operation to *Fortune* in five easy words: "Plug it in. Whirrrrrr. Done." [8]

How the iPod Got Its Name: "Open the Pod Bay Door, Hal!"

While Apple's engineers finalized the hardware, and Robbin and company worked on iTunes, a freelance copywriter was working on a name for the new device. The iPod name was offered up by Vinnie Chieco, a freelancer who lives in San Francisco, and Jobs initially rejected it.

Chieco was recruited by Apple to be part of a small team tasked with helping to figure out how to introduce the new MP3 player to the general public, not just to computer geeks. The task involved finding a name for the device, as well as creating marketing and display material to explain what it could do.

Chieco consulted with Apple for several months, sometimes meeting Jobs two or three times a week while working on the iPod. The four-man team worked in strict secrecy, meeting in a small, windowless office at the top of the building that houses Apple's graphic design department. The room was locked electronically, and only four people had access keys, including Jobs. The room had a big meeting table and a couple of computers. Some of their ideas were posted up on the walls.

The graphic design department is charged with designing Apple's product packaging, brochures, trade-show banners, and store signage, among many other things. The graphics department has a privileged position within Apple's organization: it often finds out about Apple's secret products well in advance of launch. To preserve secrecy, Apple is highly compartmentalized. Like a covert government agency, employees are given information on a strictly need-to-know-basis. Various departments know bits and pieces about new products, but only the executive team is furnished with all the details.

To prepare packaging and signage materials, artists and designers in the graphics department are often the first to learn new product details, after the executive team. The graphics department, for example, was one of the first groups inside Apple to learn the iPod's name, so that it could prepare the packaging. The other groups working on the iPod—including the hardware and the software teams—knew the device only by its code name, "Dulcimer." Even within the graphics department, information was strictly rationed. The department has about one hundred staff, but only a small subset—about twenty or thirty people—knew of the iPod's existence at all, let alone all of its details. The rest of the department found out about the iPod when Jobs unveiled it publicly to the press in October 2001.

During the process of finding a name, Jobs settled on the player's descriptive tag line: "1,000 songs in your pocket." This descriptive tag line freed up the name from having to be explanatory; it didn't have to reference music or songs. While describing the player, Jobs constantly referred to Apple's digital hub strategy: the Mac is a hub, or central connection point, for a host of gadgets, which prompted Chieco to start thinking about hubs: objects to which other things connect.

The ultimate hub, Chieco figured, would be a spaceship. You could leave the spaceship in a smaller vessel, a pod, but you'd have to return to the mother ship to refuel and get food. Then Chieco was shown a prototype iPod, with its stark white plastic front. "As soon as I saw the white iPod, I thought '2001,'" said Chieco. "'Open the pod bay door, Hal!'"

Then it was just a matter of adding the "i" prefix, like the iMac. When Apple first started using the prefix in 1999 with the iMac, Apple said the "i" stood for "internet." But the prefix is now used across such a wide range of products—from the iPhone to iMovie software—it no longer makes as much sense. Some have suggested that the "i" is the first person, denoting the personal nature of Apple's products.

Chieco presented the name to Jobs along with several dozen alternatives written on index cards. He declined to mention any of the alternative names that were considered. As he examined the index cards one-by-one, Jobs sorted them into two piles: one for candidates, the other for rejects. The iPod card went into the reject pile. But at the end of the meeting, Jobs asked the four people present for their opinions. Chieco reached across the table and pulled the "iPod" card from the reject pile. "The way Steve had been explaining this, it made sense to me," said Chieco. "It was the perfect analogy. It was very logical. Plus, it was a good name." Jobs told Chieco he'd think about it.

After the meeting, Jobs began market testing several alternative names on people inside and outside the company whom he trusted. "He was throwing out a whole lot of names," said Chieco. "He had a lot. He started to ask around." A few days later, Jobs informed Chieco that he'd made a decision in favor of iPod. He didn't offer an explanation. He simply told Chieco: "I've been thinking about that name. I like it. It's a good name." A source at Apple, who asked not be to be named (because he doesn't want to be fired), confirmed Chieco's story.

Athol Foden, a naming expert and president of Brighter Naming of Mountain View, California, noted that Apple had already trademarked the iPod name on July 24, 2000, for an Internet kiosk, a project that never saw the light of day. Apple registered the iPod name for "a public internet kiosk enclosure containing computer equipment," according to the filing.

Foden noted that the name "iPod" makes more sense for an Internet kiosk, which is a pod for a human, than a music player. "They discovered in their tool chest of registered names they had 'iPod,'" he said. "If you think about the product, it doesn't really fit. But it doesn't matter. It's short and sweet."

Foden said the name is a stroke of genius: It is simple, memorable, and, crucially, doesn't describe the device, so it can still be used as the technology evolves, even if the device's function changes. He also noted the double meaning of the "i" prefix: "internet," as in "iMac," or the first person "I," as in me.

Chieco was puzzled when I told him that Apple had already registered the iPod name. He wasn't aware of it, and neither, apparently, was Steve Jobs. Chieco said the Internet kiosk must be a coincidence. He suggested that maybe another team at Apple registered the name for a different project, but because of the company's penchant for secrecy, no one was aware that it was already one of their trademarks.

On October 23, 2001, about five weeks after the events of 9/11, Jobs introduced the finished product at a special event at Apple's HQ. "This is a major, major breakthrough," Jobs told the assembled reporters.

And so it was. The original iPod looks primitive now: a big white cigarette box with a blocky black and white screen. But every six months Apple improved, updated, and expanded the device, which culminated in a family of different models, from the bare-bones Shuffle to the luxurious iPhone.

The result: more than 100 million sold by April 2007, which accounts for just under half of Apple's ballooning revenues. Apple is on track to sell more than 200 million iPods by the end of 2008 and 300 million by the close of 2009. Some analysts think the iPod could sell 500 million units before the market is saturated. All of which would make the iPod a contender for the biggest consumer electronics hit of all time. The current record holder, Sony's Walkman, sold 350 million units during its fifteen-year reign in the 1980s and early 1990s.

Perhaps the most important aspect of the iPod's success is the total control Jobs exercised over the device: hardware, software, and online music store. The total control is key to the iPod's function, ease of use, and reliability. And it will be critical to Apple's future in the exploding digital entertainment era, as we'll see in the next chapter.

Lessons from Steve

- *If you miss the boat, work hard to catch up.* Jobs initially failed to see the digital music revolution but soon caught up.
- *Seek out opportunities.* Apple wasn't in the gadgets business, but Jobs was curious to see if there were openings.
- *Look for "vectors going in time"—bigger changes in the wider world that can be used to your advantage.* The iPod greatly benefited from improvements in batteries and screens driven by the cell phone industry.

- *Set a deadline.* Jobs wanted the iPod in stores by the fall. That was only six months to bring it to market. Punishing but necessary.
- *Don't worry where the ideas come from.* Phil Schiller, the head of Apple's marketing, suggested the iPod's scroll wheel. Other companies wouldn't even have marketing staff in a product development meeting.
- *Don't worry where the tech comes from—it's the combination that matters.* The iPod is more than a sum of its parts.
- *Leverage your expertise.* Never start from scratch—Apple's power-supply team fixed the battery, while programmers created the interface. Six months to market would have been impossible if Apple had reinvented the wheel.
- *Trust your process.* The iPod wasn't a sudden flash of genius or a breakthrough idea. It emerged from Apple's tried-and-true iterative design process.
- *Don't be afraid of trial and error.* Like Jonny Ive's endless prototypes, the iPod's breakthrough interface was discovered through a process of trial and error.
- *Embrace the team.* The iPod doesn't have a sole progenitor: there's no single "Podfather." It's never just one person—success always has many fathers.

Chapter 8

Total Control:
The Whole Widget

"I've always wanted to own and control the primary technology in everything we do."

—Steve Jobs

I n 1984, Steve Jobs's baby—the first Macintosh computer—shipped without an internal cooling fan. The sound of a fan drove Jobs nuts, so he insisted the Mac didn't have one, even though his engineers strenuously objected (and even sneaked fans into later models without his knowledge). To prevent their machines' overheating, customers bought a "Mac chimney"—a cardboard stovepipe designed to be placed on top of the machine and draw heat up and out by convection. The chimney looked preposterous—it looked like a dunce's cap—but it prevented the machines from melting down.

Jobs is a no-compromise perfectionist, a quality that has

led him and the companies he's founded to pursue the same unusual modus operandi: maintain tight control over hardware, software, and the services they access. From the get-go, Jobs has always closed down his machines. From the first Mac to the latest iPhone, Jobs's systems have always been sealed shut to prevent consumers from meddling and modifying them. Even his software is difficult to adapt.

This approach is very unusual in an industry dominated by hackers and engineers who like to personalize their technology. In fact, it's been widely regarded as a crippling liability in the Microsoft-dominated era of cut-price commodity hardware. But now consumers want well-made, easy-to-use devices for digital music, photography, and video. Jobs's insistence on controlling "the whole widget" is the new mantra in the technology industry. Even Microsoft's Bill Gates, who pioneered the commodity approach, is switching gears and emulating Jobs's line of attack. Gates is starting to build hardware as well as software— with Microsoft's Zune and the Xbox at the heart of Microsoft's own "digital hub." Controlling the whole widget may have been the wrong model for the last thirty years, but it is the right model for the next thirty—the digital entertainment age.

In this new era, Hollywood and the music industry are supplementing CDs and DVDs with Internet delivery of music and movies, and consumers want easy-to-use entertainment appliances like the iPod to play them on. It's Steve Jobs's model that will deliver them. Apple's trump card is that it is able to make its own software, from the Mac operating system to applications such as iPhoto and iTunes.

Jobs as a Control Freak

Jobs is a control-freak extraordinaire. He controls Apple's software, hardware, and design. He controls Apple's marketing and online services. He controls every aspect of the organization's functioning, from the food the employees eat to how much they can tell their families about their work, which is pretty much nothing.

Before Jobs returned to Apple, the company was famously laid back. Employees arrived late and left early. They lounged around the grassy central courtyard, playing hacky-sack or throwing Frisbees to their dogs. But Jobs soon imposed new rigor and new rules. Smoking and dogs were barred, and the company had a renewed sense of urgency and industry.

Some have suggested that Jobs keeps tight control at Apple to avoid being ousted again. The last time he ceded control to his supposed friend and ally, John Sculley, Sculley had him expelled from the company. Perhaps, some have speculated, Jobs's controlling tendencies are a result of his being adopted as a child. His controlling personality is a reaction to the helplessness of being abandoned by his birth parents. But as we've seen, Jobs's control-freak tendencies have lately turned out to be good business, and good for the design of consumer-friendly gadgets. Tight control of hardware and software pays dividends in ease of use, security, and reliability.

Whatever their origins, Jobs's control-freak tendencies are the stuff of legend. In the early days of Apple, Jobs fought with his friend and cofounder, Steve Wozniak, who strongly advocated open, accessible machines. Wozniak, the ultimate hackers' hacker, wanted computers that were easy to open and adapt. Jobs wanted the precise opposite: machines that were locked shut and impossible to modify. The first Macs, which Jobs oversaw mostly without Wozniak's help, were tightly sealed with special screws that could be loosened only with a proprietary foot-long screwdriver.

More recently, Jobs locked software developers out of the iPhone, at least initially. In the weeks following Jobs's introduction of the iPhone, there was a storm of protest from bloggers and pundits who furiously ranted and raved that the iPhone would be a closed platform. It wouldn't run software from anyone but Apple. The iPhone was poised to be one of the hottest consumer electronics platforms in recent memory, but it was forbidden fruit to the software industry. Third-party applications were verboten, except web applications running on the phone's browser. Many critics said locking out developers this way was typical of Jobs's controlling tendencies. He didn't want grubby outside programmers wrecking the perfect Zen of his device.

"Jobs is a strong-willed, elitist artist who doesn't want to see his creations mutated inauspiciously by unworthy program-mers," wrote Dan Farber, ZDNet's editor in chief. "It would be as if someone off the street added some brush strokes to a Pi-casso painting or changed the lyrics to a Bob Dylan song."[1]

Critics said barring third-party software was a critical mis-take. It would cost the iPhone its killer app—the crucial piece of software that would make it a must-have device. In the his-tory of the PC, successful hardware has often been determined by an exclusive piece of software: VisiCalc on the Apple II, Al-dus Pagemaker and desktop publishing on the Mac, Halo on the Xbox.

Jobs's strategy of keeping the iPod/iTunes ecosystem closed to partners was also seen by pundits as another example of his desire to maintain complete control. Critics have argued that Jobs should license iTunes to competitors, which would allow songs bought online from the iTunes music store to be played on MP3 players made by other manufacturers. As it is, songs bought from iTunes can be played only on iPods because of copy protection code attached to song files, known as Digital Rights Management, or DRM.

Others have argued that Jobs should do the opposite: open the iPod to Microsoft's competing Windows Media format. WMA is the default file format for music files on Windows PCs. CDs ripped on a Windows PC, or bought from an online store like Napster or Virgin Digital, are usually encoded as WMA files. (The iPod and iTunes currently import WMA files and convert them to the iPod's format of choice: AAC.)

Predictably, some critics argued that Jobs's refusal to open the iPod or iTunes to Microsoft's formats or outside partners was because of Jobs's long-seated need to maintain absolute control. Rob Glaser, founder and CEO of RealNetworks, which operates the rival Rhapsody music service, told the *New York Times* that Jobs was sacrificing commercial logic in the name of "ideology." Speaking in 2003, Glaser said: "It's absolutely clear now why five years from now, Apple will have 3 to 5 percent of the player market.... The history of the world is that hybridization yields better results."[2]

Glaser and other critics could see a clear parallel to the Windows versus Mac war of old: Apple's refusal to license the Mac cost the company its massive early lead in the computer market. While Microsoft licensed its operating system to all comers and quickly grew to a dominant position, Apple kept its toys to itself. Even though the Mac was much more advanced than Windows, it was doomed to a tiny sliver of the market.

Some critics have argued that the same thing would happen with the iPod and iTunes, that Jobs's refusal to play nice with others would result in Apple's getting the same trouncing in digital music that it received in the PC business. Observers argued that eventually an open system licensed to all comers, like Microsoft's PlaysForSure, which was adopted by dozens of online music stores and manufacturers of MP3 players, would trump Apple's go-it-alone approach. Critics said Apple would be faced with the fierce competition that naturally arises from an open market. Competing manufacturers, trying to outdo one another on price and features, would constantly drive down prices while improving their devices.

Apple, on the other hand, would be locked into its own cuckoo land of expensive players able to play songs only from its own store. To critics, it was the classic Steve Jobs play: his desire to keep it for himself would doom the iPod. Microsoft, with its legions of partners, would do the same thing to the iPod that it did to the Mac.

And again, the same criticisms were leveled with the release of the iPhone, which was initially closed to outside software developers. The iPhone ran a handful of applications from Apple and Google—Google Maps, iPhoto, iCal—but was not open to third-party developers.

The hunger for developers to get their programs on the device was evident from the start. Within days of its release, the iPhone had been opened up by enterprising hackers, allowing owners to upload applications to the phone. Within weeks, more than two hundred applications had been developed for the iPhone, including clever location finders and innovative games.

But the application hack depended on a security weakness, which Apple quickly closed with a software update. The update also closed holes that had allowed some iPhone owners—in fact, quite a lot of them—to "unlock" their phones from AT&T's network and use them with other wireless providers. (Apple revealed that as many as 25,000 iPhones hadn't been registered with AT&T, suggesting that nearly one in six phones sold were being used with other providers, many likely overseas.)

The update disabled some iPhones, in particular ones that had been hacked. This appears to be unintentional on Apple's part, but the "bricking" of so many devices turned into a PR nightmare. For many commentators, customers, and bloggers, it was Apple at its worst: treating early adopters and loyal customers like dirt, disabling their devices because they had the temerity to mess with them.

The developer community also reacted with shock and outrage, accusing Apple of blowing an opportunity to get an early lead on rivals like Microsoft, Google, Nokia, and Symbian in the smartphone market. To assuage the outrage, Apple announced a plan to open up the iPhone to third-party developers in February 2008 with a software developer's kit.

Controlling the Whole Widget

Jobs's desire to control the whole widget is both philosophical and practical. It's not just control for control's sake. Jobs wants to make complex devices like computers and smartphones into truly mass-market products, and to do that, he believes that Apple needs to wrest control of the devices partly from the consumer. The iPod is a good example. The complexities of managing an MP3 player are hidden from the consumer by having iTunes software and the iTunes store manage the experience.

No, consumers can't buy tunes from any online store they like, but then the iPod doesn't freeze up when music is transferred onto it. This is the practical aspect. The tight integration of hardware and software makes for a more manageable, predictable system. A closed system limits choice, but it is more stable and more reliable. An open system is far more fragile and unreliable—this is the price of freedom.

Jobs's desire to build closed systems can be traced all the way back to the original Mac. In the early days of the PC, computers were notoriously unreliable. They were prone to constant crashes, freezes, and reboots. Users were just as likely to lose hours of work on a document as they were of successfully printing it. This was as true of Apple's computers as it was of computers from IBM, Compaq, or Dell.

One of the biggest problems was expansion slots, which allowed owners to upgrade and expand their machines with extra hardware like new graphics cards, networking boards, and fax/modems. The slots were popular with businesses and electronics hobbyists, who expected to be able to customize their machines. For many of these customers, that was the point: they wanted computers that could easily be hacked for their purposes. But these expansion slots also made early computers notoriously unstable. The problem was that each piece of add-on hardware needed its own driver software to make it work with the computer's operating system. Driver software helps the operating system recognize the hardware and sends commands to it, but it can also cause conflicts with other soft-

ware, leading to lockups. Worse, drivers were often badly pro-
grammed: they were buggy and unreliable, especially in the
early days.

In 1984, Jobs and the Mac development team decided they
would try to bring an end to the crashes and freezes. They decided that the Mac wouldn't have expansion slots. If it couldn't
be expanded, it wouldn't suffer from these driver conflicts. To
make sure there was no tinkering, the case was locked shut
with proprietary screws that couldn't be loosened with an ordinary screwdriver.

Critics saw this as a clear indication of Jobs's control-freak
tendencies. Not only was his machine unexpandable, he physi-
cally locked it shut. Jobs had boasted of his desire that the Mac
would be the "perfect machine," and here he was ensuring it.
The Mac's perfection would survive even after it was shipped to
users. It was locked shut to protect them from themselves: they
wouldn't be able to ruin it.

But the idea wasn't to punish users; it was to make the Mac
more stable and less buggy, and to enable programs to be integrated with each other. "The goal of keeping the system closed
had to do with ending the chaos that had existed on the earlier
machines," said Daniel Kottke, a teenage friend of Jobs's and
one of Apple's first employees.[3]

Additionally, the lack of expansion slots allowed the hardware to be simplified and cheaper to manufacture. The Mac
was already going to be an expensive machine; eliminating expansion cards would make it a little bit cheaper.

But it turned out to be a wrong decision at the dawn of the fast-moving PC industry. As Andy Hertzfeld, the whiz kid programmer on the original Mac development team, explained: "The biggest problem with the Macintosh hardware was pretty obvious, which was its limited expandability," Hertzfeld wrote. "But the problem wasn't really technical as much as philosophical, which was that we wanted to eliminate the inevitable complexity that was a consequence of hardware expandability, both for the user and the developer, by having every Macintosh be identical. It was a valid point of view, even somewhat courageous, but not very practical, because things were still changing too fast in the computer industry for it to work."[4]

The Virtues of Control Freakery: Stability, Security, and Ease-of-Use

These days, most of Apple's machines are expandable. Computers at the high end of Apple's range have several expansion slots. Thanks to new programming tools and certification programs, which require rigorous testing, software drivers are much better behaved on both Macs and Windows. And yet Macs enjoy a much better reputation for stability than Windows computers.

Modern Macs use much the same components as Windows PCs. The guts are almost identical, from the central Intel processor to the RAM. Same is true of the hard drives, video cards, PCI slots, and the chipsets for USB, WiFi, and Bluetooth. The internal components of most computers are interchangeable, whether they come from Dell, HP, or Apple. As a result, the computer business is a lot less incompatible than it used to be. Many peripherals like printers or webcams are compatible with both platforms. Microsoft's Intellimouse plugs right into a Mac, and it works instantly and flawlessly.

The biggest difference between the Mac and the PC is the operating system. Apple is the last company in the industry that still has control of its own software. Dell and HP license their operating systems from Microsoft. The problem is that Microsoft's operating system must support hundreds—maybe thousands—of different hardware components, assembled in potentially millions of different ways. Apple has it much easier. Apple makes only two or three major lines of computer, most of which share common components. The Mac mini, iMac, and MacBook are all basically the same computer in different packages.

From this perspective, Windows is an extraordinary achievement of engineering. The range and scope of the hardware it runs on is quite impressive. But there are so many variables that it can't hope to provide the same level of compatibility and stability. Microsoft's major initiative to make hardware more compatible—Plug and Play—became known as Plug and Pray because there were so many combinations of hardware and software and the results were unpredictable.

Apple, on the other hand, has a much smaller hardware base to support, and the results are much more predictable. In addition, if something goes wrong, there's only one company to call. Customers of Dell or Compaq dread phone-support hell, where the hardware maker blames Microsoft, and Microsoft blames the hardware maker.

"PlaysForShit". Take Microsoft's music system PlaysForSure, launched in 2005. Licensed to dozens of online music companies and manufacturers of portable players, PlaysForSure was supposed to be an iPod killer. It would offer more competition and better prices. Trouble is, it was unbelievably unreliable.

I had several of my own nightmare experiences with it. I knew there were problems, but I was truly shocked at how crappy it was. In 2006, Amazon.com introduced a video download service called Amazon Unbox. Launched to great fanfare, the service promised hundreds of movies and TV shows "on demand," which could be quickly and easily downloaded to a PC hard drive with a single click. The service promised that video could be copied to PlaysForSure devices like an 8-Gigabyte SanDisk player I was testing.

Actually, Amazon didn't promise its video would play on PlaysForSure devices; it said video *might* play on PlaysForSure devices. "If your device is PlaysForSure-compliant, it may work," said Amazon's website. *May* work? Surely this was a joke? The point of PlaysForSure was that media would play for sure. Alas, it didn't. After fiddling with it for hours, plugging and unplugging the player, restarting the PC, reinstalling software, and searching the Web for tips, I gave up. Life's too short.

The problem is that Microsoft makes the software that runs on the computer, but SanDisk makes the software that controls the player. Over time, Microsoft made several upgrades to its PlaysForSure software to fix bugs and security problems, but to work properly with the new software, SanDisk players also had to be updated. While Microsoft and SanDisk tried to coordinate the updates, there were sometimes conflicts and delays. The more companies involved, the more the problems confounded. Microsoft struggled to support dozens of online stores and dozens of player manufacturers who, in turn, had shipped dozens of different models. Hardware companies had a hard time persuading Microsoft to fix PlaysForSure problems, which included glitches transferring subscription songs and even failures to recognize connected players. "We can't get them to fix the bugs," Anu Kirk, a director at Real, told CNet.[5]

In addition, all the troubleshooting had to be performed by the user, who had to seek out the latest updates and install them.

Apple, on the other hand, was able to issue similar upgrades to tens of millions of iPods quickly and efficiently through its iTunes software. If there was a new version of the iPod software, iTunes would automatically update the iPod when it was plugged into the computer—with the user's consent, of course. It was, and is, a highly efficient, automated system. There's only one software application and, essentially, one device to support (even though there are several different models).

At the time, there was a lot of criticism of Apple's growing monopoly of the online music market and the tight integration between the iPod and iTunes. And while I object intellectually to being locked into Apple's system, at least it works. I've used an iPod for several years, and it's easy to forget how seamless the iPod experience is. It's only when things go wrong with your gadgets that you stop and take notice. In the years I've been using an iPod, I've never had a problem—no lost files, no failure to sync, no breakdown of battery or hard drive.

Stability and User Experience: The iPhone. One of the big selling points for the Mac is the suite of iLife applications: iTunes, iPhoto, Garageband, and the like. The apps are designed for everyday creative activities: storing and organizing digital photos; making home movies; recording songs to post to MySpace.

The iLife apps are a big part of what makes the Mac a Mac. There's nothing like it on Windows. Steve Jobs often points this out as a differentiating feature. It's like an exclusive version of Microsoft Office that's available only on the Mac, but it's for fun, creative projects, not work.

One of iLife's selling points is that the applications are tightly integrated with each other. The photo application, iPhoto, is aware of all the music stored in iTunes, which makes it easy to add a soundtrack to photo slideshows. The homepage building application, iWeb, can access all the pictures in iPhoto, which makes uploading photos to an online gallery a two-click process. Integration on the Mac is not limited to the iLife suite, however. Across the board, much of Apple's software is integrated: Address Book is integrated with iCal which is integrated with iSync which is integrated with Address Book, and so on. This level of interoperability is unique to Apple. Microsoft's Office suite offers a similar level of integration, but it is restricted to the productivity apps that ship with Office. It's not systemwide.

The same philosophy of integration and ease of use extends to the iPhone. Jobs took a lot of criticism for closing the iPhone to outside developers, but he did so to ensure stability, security, and ease of use. "You don't want your phone to be an open platform," Jobs explained to *Newsweek*. "You need it to work when you need it to work. Cingular [not AT&T] doesn't want to see their West Coast network go down because some application messed up."[6]

While Jobs is exaggerating that one unruly app will take down a cell network, it can certainly take down a single phone. Just look what the open-platform approach has done to Windows (and, yes, Mac OS X, too, to a lesser extent)—it's a world of viruses, Trojans, and spyware. How to avoid? Make the iPhone closed. Jobs's motivation is not aesthetics, but user experience. To ensure the best user experience, the software, hardware, and services users access will be tightly integrated. While some see this as lockdown, to Jobs it's the difference between the pleasure of the iPhone and the pain of a confusing off-brand cell phone. I'll take the iPhone. Because Apple controls the whole widget, it can offer better stability, better integration, and faster innovation.

Devices will work well if they are designed to work well together, and it's easier to add new features if all parts of a system are developed under the same roof. Samsung's TVs don't crash because Samsung takes care of the software as well as the hardware. TiVo does the same.

Of course, Apple's iPhone/iPod/iTunes system is not perfect. It too crashes, freezes, and wipes files. The integration of Apple's apps offers a lot of benefits, but it means that Apple is sometimes too inwardly focused when better services come along. For many people, Flickr offers a better experience for uploading and sharing photos, but users need to download a third-party plug-in to make it as easy as uploading photos to Apple's web services. Macs still crash and peripherals can go unrecognized when plugged in—but in general, their stability and compatibility are better than Windows'. Thanks to Jobs's control freakery.

The Systems Approach

Jobs's desire to control the whole widget has had an unexpected consequence, which has led Apple to a fundamentally new way of creating products. Instead of making stand-alone computers and gadgets, Apple now makes whole business systems.

Jobs first got a peek at this systems approach in 2000 while developing iMovie 2. The application was one of the first consumer-friendly video-editing applications on the market. The software was designed to let people take footage from a camcorder and turn it into a polished piece of filmmaking with edits, fades, a soundtrack, and credits. With subsequent versions, movies could be posted on the Web or burned to DVD to share with Grandma.

Jobs was delighted with the software—he's a lover of digital video—but soon realized that iMovie's magic wasn't conjured up by the software alone. To function properly, the software had to be used in conjunction with several other components: a fast plug-and-play connection to the camcorder; an operating system that recognized the camera and made an automatic connection; and a suite of underlying multimedia software that provided video codes and real-time video effects (QuickTime). It occurred to Jobs that there weren't many companies left in the PC business that had all these elements.

"We realized Apple was uniquely suited to do this because we are the last company in this business that has all the components under one roof," Jobs said at Macworld in 2001. "We think it's a unique strength and we discovered this with iMovie, that it could make a digital device like a camcorder worth ten times as much. It has ten times as much value to you."

After shipping iMovie, Jobs turned his attention from digital video to digital music, and he forged the biggest breakthrough of his career. The best example of Jobs's new systems approach is the iPod, which isn't a stand-alone music player, but a combination of gadget, computer, iTunes software, and online music store.

"I think the definition of product has changed over the decades," said Tony Fadell, senior vice president of the iPod Division, who led the hardware development of the original iPod. "The product now is the iTunes Music Store and iTunes and the iPod and the software that goes on the iPod. A lot of companies don't really have control, or they can't really work in a collaborative way to truly make a system. We're really about a system."[7]

In the early days of the iPod, many expected Apple would soon be overtaken by competitors. The press was constantly touting the latest "iPod killer." But until Microsoft's Zune came along, each device was essentially a stand-alone player. Apple's competitors were focusing on the gadget, not the software and services that supported it.

Apple's former head of hardware, Jon Rubinstein, who oversaw development of the first several generations of the iPod, is skeptical that competitors can overtake the iPod any time soon. Some critics had likened the iPod to Sony's Walkman, which was eventually eclipsed by cheaper knock-offs. But Rubinstein said it is unlikely the iPod would suffer the same fate. "The iPod is substantially more difficult to copy than that Walkman was," he said. "It contains a whole ecosystem of different elements, which coordinate with each other: hardware, software, and our iTunes Music store on the Internet."[8]

These days, most of Apple's products are similar combinations of hardware, software, and online services. The AppleTV, which connects computers to TVs via WiFi, is another combo product: it's the box that's wired to the TV, the software that connects it to other computers around the house—both Macs and Windows PCs—and the iTunes software and store for buying and downloading TV shows and movies. The iPhone is the phone handset, the iTunes software that syncs it with a computer, and network services like Visual Voicemail, which make it easy to check messages.

Several of Apple's iLife applications connect to the Net. Apple's photo software, iPhoto, can share pictures over the Net via a mechanism called "photocasting," or order prints or photo books online. iMovie has an export function for posting home movies to homepages; Apple's backup app can save critical data online; and its iSync software uses the Net to synchronize calendar and contact information among multiple computers. None of this is unique to Apple, of course, but few companies have embraced the hardware, software, and services model so comprehensively or effectively.

The Return of Vertical Integration

Apple's competitors are starting to wise up to the virtues of vertical integration, or a whole-systems approach. In August

2006, Nokia acquired Loudeye, a music licensing company that built several "white label" music stores for other companies. Nokia bought Loudeye to kickstart its own iTunes service for its multimedia phones and handsets.

In 2006, RealNetworks teamed up with SanDisk, the number-two player manufacturer in the United States behind Apple, to pair their hardware and software offerings à la the iPod. Cutting out the middleman—Microsoft's PlaysForSure—the companies instead opted for Real's Helix digital rights management, which promised tighter integration.

Sony, which has decades of hardware expertise but little or none in software, has set up a software group in California to coordinate development across the giant's disparate product groups.

The group is run by Tim Schaaff, a former Apple executive, who has been anointed Sony's "software czar." Schaff has been charged with developing a consistent, distinctive software platform for Sony's many products. He will also try to foster collaboration between disparate product groups, each of which works in its own "silo." At Sony, there's historically been little cross pollination between isolated product groups, and there's a lot of repeated effort but little interoperability.

Sir Howard Stringer, Sony's first non-Japanese CEO, reorganized the company and empowered Schaaff's software development group to address these problems. "There's no question that the iPod was a wakeup call for Sony," Sir Howard told CBS's 60 *Minutes*. "And the answer is that Steve Jobs [is] smarter at software than we are."

Most significantly, Microsoft abandoned its own PlaysForSure system in favor of the Zune, a combination player, digital jukebox, and online store.

Although Microsoft pledged to continue to support PlaysForSure, its decision to go with its new vertically integrated Zune music system was a clear message that its horizontal approach had failed.

The Zune and Xbox

The Zune comes out of Microsoft's Entertainment & Devices Division, a unique hardware/software shop that technology journalist Walt Mossberg characterized as a "small Apple" inside Microsoft.[9] Run by Robbie Bach, a Microsoft vet who rose through the ranks, the division is responsible for the Zune music players and Xbox game consoles. Like Apple, it develops its own hardware and software, and runs the online stores and community services that its devices connect to. In spring 2007, the division unveiled a new product, an interactive, touchscreen tabletop called Surface.

The division has in its sights Sony and Nintendo, as well as Apple, and is pursuing a strategy it calls "connected entertainment"—"new and compelling, branded entertainment experiences across music, gaming, video and mobile communications," according to Microsoft's website.

"It's the idea that your media, whether it's music, video, photos, games, whatever—you should have access to that wherever you are and on whatever device you want—a PC, an Xbox, a Zune, a phone, whatever works and in whatever room it works," Bach told the *San Francisco Chronicle*. "In order to do that, Microsoft has taken assets from across the company and consolidated them in this division.... We're working on the specific areas of video, music, gaming and mobile, and also trying to work to make all those things come together in a coherent, logical way."[10]

But to make it work in a coherent, logical way, one company has to control all the components. In technology jargon, this is known as "vertical integration."

When the *Chronicle* asked Bach to compare Apple's and Microsoft's approaches to consumer devices—horizontal versus vertical integration—Bach danced about a little, before acknowledging the strengths of his competitor's approach. "In some markets," he said, "the benefits of choice and breadth play out successfully. On the other hand, there [are] other markets and what people are really looking for is the ease of use of a vertically integrated solution. And what Apple demonstrated with its iPod is that a vertically integrated solution could be successful in a mass way." Bach admitted that his division is adopting Apple's "vertically integrated" model: it is blending hardware, software, and online services. "The market showed that's what consumers want," he said.

What Consumers Want

These days, more and more technology companies talk not about products, but "solutions" or "customer experiences." Microsoft's press release announcing the Zune music player was entitled: "Microsoft to Put Zune Experience in Consumers' Hands on Nov 14." The release emphasized not the player, but a seamless customer experience, including connecting to other music lovers online and off, via the Zune's WiFi sharing capabilities. It was "an end-to-end solution for connected entertainment," Microsoft said.

The market research firm Forrester Research published a paper in December 2005: "Sell digital experiences, not products." Forrester pointed out that consumers spend a fortune on expensive new toys, like big high-definition TVs, but then they fail to buy the services or content that bring them to life, like high-definition cable service. The firm recommended: "To close this gap, digital industries must stop selling standalone devices and services and start delivering digital experiences— products and services integrated end-to-end under the control of a single application."[11] Sound familiar?

In September 2007, at a special press event in San Francisco, Steve Jobs leapt on stage with a big grin to introduce the iPod touch: the first finger-controlled iPod. During the ninety-minute presentation, Jobs unveiled a cornucopia of Christmas goodies, including a completely revamped line of iPods and a WiFi music store coming to thousands of Starbucks coffee shops.

Industry analyst Tim Bajarin, president of Creative Strategies, who's followed the tech industry for decades and has seen it all, is not easily bowled over. Nonetheless, after Jobs's presentation as he stood in the aisle talking to reporters, Bajarin was shaking his head in disbelief. Ticking off the items one by one—new iPods, the WiFi music store, the Starbucks partnership—Bajarin noted that Apple had a full lineup of killer gadgets at every price point and a comprehensive media delivery system. "I don't know how Microsoft and the Zune competes with something like that," he said. "The industrial design, the pricing models that set new rules, the innovation, WiFi." Now he was shaking his head more vigorously. "It's not just Microsoft. Who out there has the ability to compete with that?"

In the thirty years since founding Apple, Jobs has remained remarkably consistent. The demand for excellence, the pursuit of great design, the instinct for marketing, the insistence on ease of use and compatibility, all have been there from the get-go. It's just that they were the right instincts at the wrong time.

In the early days of the computer industry—the era of mainframes and centralized data processing centers—vertical integration was the name of the game. The giants of the mainframe business, IBM, Honeywell, and Burroughs, sent in armies of button-down consultants who researched, designed, and built the systems. They built IBM hardware and installed IBM software, and then ran, maintained, and repaired the systems on the customer's behalf. For technophobic corporations of the sixties and seventies, vertical integration worked well enough, but it meant being locked into one company's system.

But then the computer industry matured and it disaggregated. Companies started to specialize. Intel and National Semiconductor made chips, Compaq and HP made computers, and Microsoft provided the software. The industry grew, spurring competition, greater choice, and ever-falling prices. Customers could pick and choose hardware and software from different companies. They ran databases from Oracle on top of hardware from IBM.

Only Apple stuck to its whole-widget guns. Apple remained the last—and only—vertically integrated computer company. All the other vertical integrators, companies that made their own hardware and software—Commodore, Amiga, and Olivetti—are long gone.

In the early days, controlling the whole widget gave Apple an advantage in stability and ease of use, but it was soon erased by the economies of scale that came with the commoditization of the PC industry. Price and performance became more important than integration and ease of use, and Apple came close to extinction in the late nineties as Microsoft grew to dominance.

But the PC industry is changing. There's a new era opening

up that has the potential to dwarf the size and scope of the productivity era of the last thirty years. The era of digital entertainment has dawned. It's marked by post-PC gadgets and communication devices: smartphones and video players, digital cameras, set top boxes, and Net-connected game consoles.

The pundits are obsessed with the old Apple-versus-Microsoft battle for the workplace. But Jobs conceded that to Microsoft a decade ago. "The roots of Apple were to build computers for people, not for corporations," Jobs told *Time*. "The world doesn't need another Dell or Compaq."[12] Jobs has got his eye on the exploding digital entertainment market—and the iPod, iPhone, and AppleTV are digital entertainment devices. In this market, consumers want devices that are well designed and easy to use, and work in harmony. Nowadays, hardware companies must get into software, and vice versa.

Owning the whole widget is why no other company has been able to build an iPod killer. Most rivals focus on the hardware—the gadget—but the secret sauce is the seamless blend of hardware, software, and services.

Now Microsoft has two whole-widget products—the Xbox and Zune—and the consumer electronics industry is getting heavily into software. Jobs has stayed the same; the world is changing around him. "My, how times have changed," wrote Walt Mossberg. "Now, with computers, the Web and consumer electronics all merging and blurring, Apple is looking more like a role model than an object of pity."[13] The things Jobs cares about—design, ease of use, good advertising—are right in the sweet spot of the new computer industry.

"Apple's the only company left in this industry that designs the whole widget," Jobs told *Time*. "Hardware, software, developer relations, marketing. It turns out that that, in my opinion, is Apple's greatest strategic advantage. We didn't have a plan, so it looked like this was a tremendous deficit. But with a plan, it's Apple's core strategic advantage, if you believe that there's still room for innovation in this industry, which I do, because Apple can innovate faster than anyone else."[14]

Jobs was thirty years ahead of his time. The values he brought to the early PC market—design, marketing, ease of use—were the wrong values. The growth of the early PC market was selling to corporations, which valued price above elegance and standardization over ease of use. But the growth market is now digital entertainment and home consumers, who want digital entertainment, communication, creativity—three areas that play to Jobs's strengths. "The great thing is that Apple's DNA hasn't changed," Jobs said. "The place where Apple has been standing for the last two decades is exactly where computer technology and the consumer electronics markets are converging. So it's not like we're having to cross the river to go somewhere else; the other side of the river is coming to us."[15]

In a consumer market, design, reliability, simplicity, good

marketing, and elegant packaging are key assets. It's coming full circle—the company that does it all is the one best positioned to lead.

"It seems to take a very unique combination of technology, talent, business and marketing and luck to make significant change in our industry," Steve Jobs told *Rolling Stone* in 1994. "It hasn't happened that often."

Acknowledgments

Many thanks for help and support from everyone who gave their time for interviews, shared their expertise and stories, and provided encouragement and support. The list includes but is not limited to: Gordon Bell, Warren Berger, Robert Brunner, Vinnie Chieco, Traci Dauphin, Seth Godin, Evan Hansen, Nobuyuki Hayashi, Peter Hoddie, Guy Kawasaki, John Maeda, Geoffrey Moore, Bill Moggridge, Pete Mortensen, Don Norman, Jim Oliver, Cordell Ratzlaff, Jon Rubinstein, John Sculley, Adrienne Schultz, Dag Spicer, Patrick Whitney, and other sources who asked not to be named.

Special thanks to Ted Weinstein for suggesting the book and providing constant encouragement.

Notes

Introduction

1. Alan Deutschman, *The Second Coming of Steve Jobs* (New York: Broadway, 2001), pp. 59, 197, 239, 243, 254, 294–95; William L. Simon and Jeffrey S. Young, *iCon: Steve Jobs, The Greatest Second Act in the History of Business* (New York: John Wiley & Sons, 2005), pp. 212, 213, 254.
2. "Steve's Job: Restart Apple," by Cathy Booth, *Time*, Aug. 18, 1997. (http://www.time.com/time/magazine/article/0,9171,986849,00.html)
3. "Oh, Yeah, He Also Sells Computers," by John Markoff, *New York Times*, April 25, 2004.
4. Private e-mail from Gordon Bell, November 2007.
5. Smithsonian Institution Oral and Video Histories: "Steve Jobs," by David Morrow, April 20, 1995. (http://americanhistory.si.edu/collections/comphist/sj1.html)
6. "Google's Chief Looks Ahead," by Jeremy Caplan, *Time*, Oct. 2, 2006. (http://www.time.com/time/business/article/0,8599,1541446,00.html)

7. "How Big Can Apple Get?" by Brent Schlender, *Fortune*, February 21, 2005.

8. Stanford University commencement address by Steve Jobs, June 12, 2005. (http://news-service.stanford.edu/news/2005/june15/jobs-061505.html)

9. Guy Kawasaki, personal interview, 2006.

10. Gil Amelio with William L. Simon, *On the Firing Line: My 500 Days at Apple* (New York: Harper Business, 1999), Preface, p. x.

Chapter 1: Focus: How Saying "No" Saved Apple

1. "Steve Jobs' Magic Kingdom. How Apple's demanding visionary will shake up Disney and the world of entertainment," by Peter Burrows and Ronald Grover, with Heather Green in New York. *Business Week*. Feb. 6, 2006. (http://www.businessweek.com/magazine/content/06_06/b3970001.htm)

2. "IBM had a 10.8 percent market share; Apple 9.4 percent; and Compaq Computer 8.1 percent, according to market research firm IDC," *New York Times*, Jan. 26, 1995, Vol. 144, No. 49953.

3. "Apple's Executive Mac Math: The Greater the Lows, the Greater the Salary," by Denise Carreso, *New York Times*, July 14, 1997.

4. Amelio with Simon, *On the Firing Line*, p. 192.

5. Ibid., p. 193.

6. Ibid., p. 199.

7. "Steve's Job: Restart Apple."

8. In the first quarter of 1996, Apple recorded a loss of $740 million.

9. Amelio with Simon, *On the Firing Line*, p. 200.

10. Ibid., p. 198.

11. Apple's World Wide Developers Conference, May 11, 1998.

12. Don Norman, personal interview, October 2006.

13. Deutschman, *The Second Coming of Steve Jobs*, p. 256.

14. Jim Oliver, personal interview, October 2006.

15. Oliver said he was later amazed that Apple's revenues did indeed bottom out at about $5.4 billion.

16. "Steve's Job: Restart Apple."

17. Ibid.

18. Ibid.

19. "Steve Jobs' Magic Kingdom."

20. Ibid.

21. "The Three Faces of Steve. In this exclusive, personal conversation, Apple's CEO reflects on the turnaround, and on how a wunderkind became an old pro," by Brent Schlender and Steve Jobs, *Fortune*, Nov. 9, 1998. (http://money.cnn.com/magazines/fortune/fortune__archive/1998/11/09/250880/index.htm)

22. "Steve's Job: Restart Apple."

23. Jim Oliver, personal interview, October 2006.

24. Seybold San Francisco/Publishing '98, Web Publishing Conference, special keynote: Steve Jobs, Aug. 31, 1998.

25. "Steve Jobs on Apple's Resurgence: 'Not a One-Man Show'," by Andy Reinhart, *Business Week Online*, May 12, 1998. (http://www.businessweek.com/bwdaily/dnflash/may1998/nf80512d.htm)

26. "Gates Takes a Swipe at iMac," CNET News.com staff, July 26, 1999. (http://www.news.com/Gates-takes-a-swipe-at-iMac/2100-1001_3-229037.html)

27. "Thinking Too Different," by Hiawatha Bray, *Boston Globe*, May 14, 1998.

28. "Stringer: Content Drives Digitization," by Georg Szalai, *The Hollywood Reporter*, Nov. 9, 2007. (http://www.hollywoodreporter.com/hr/content__display/business/news/e3idd293825dd51c45cff4f1036c8398c0e)

29. "The Music Man: Apple CEO Steve Jobs Talks About the Success of iTunes, Mac's Future, Movie Piracy," by Walter S. Mossberg, *Wall Street Journal*, June 14, 2004. (http://online.wsj.com/article__email/SB108716565680435835-IRjfYNolaV3nZyqaHmHcKmGm4.html)

30. Ibid.

31. "Steve Jobs at 44," by Michael Krantz and Steve Jobs, *Time*, Oct. 10, 1999.

32. IDC, Top 5 Vendors, United States PC Shipments, Third Quarter 2007. (http://www.idc.com/getdoc.jsp;jsessionid=Z53BVCY1DTP R2CQJAFICFGAKBEAUMIWD?containerId=prUS20914007)

Chapter 2: Despotism: Apple's One-Man Focus Group

1. Cordell Ratzlaff, personal interview, September 2006.

2. Peter Hoddie, personal interview, September 2006.

3. "Steve Jobs: The Rolling Stone Interview. He changed the computer industry. Now he's after the music business," by Jeff Goodell, posted Dec. 3, 2003. (http://www.rollingstone.com/news/ story/5939600/steve__jobs__the__rolling__stone__interview)

4. "The Guts of a New Machine," by Rob Walker, *New York Times Magazine*, Nov. 30, 2003. (http://www.nytimes.com/2003/11/30/ magazine/30IPOD.html)

5. Ibid.

6. John Sculley, personal interview, December 2007.

7. Ibid.

8. Patrick Whitney, personal interview, October 2006.

9. "Steve Jobs on Apple's Resurgence."

10. Dag Spicer, personal Interview, October 2006.

11. Guy Kawasaki, personal interview, October 2006.

Chapter 3: Perfectionism: Product Design and the Pursuit of Excellence

1. "Steve's Two Jobs," by Michael Krantz, *Time*, Oct. 10, 1999. (http:// www.time.com/time/magazine/article/0,9171,32209-2,00.html)

2. Paul Kunkel and Rick English, *Apple Design: The Work of the Apple Industrial Design Group* (Watson-Guptill Publications, 1997), p. 22.

3. Ibid., p. 13.

4. Ibid.

5. Ibid., p. 15.

6. Ibid., pp. 28–37.

7. Ibid., p. 26.

8. Andy Hertzfeld, *Revolution in the Valley* (Sebastapol, Calif.: O'Reilly Media, 2004), p. 30.

9. "Signing Party," Andy Hertzfeld, Folklore.org. (http://www .folklore.org/StoryView.py?project=Macintosh&story=Signing__ Party.txt&showcomments=1)

10. Quoted in Steven Levy, *Insanely Great: The Life and Times of Macintosh, the Computer That Changed Everything* (New York: Penguin, 1994), p. 186.

11. "Why We Buy: Interview with Jonathan Ive," by Charles Fishman, *Fast Company*, Oct. 1999, p. 282. (http://www.fastcompany.com/ magazine/29/buy.html)

12. Ibid.

13. "PC Board Esthetics," by Andy Hertzfeld, Folklore.org (http://www .folklore.org/StoryView.py?project=Macintosh&story=PC__ Board__Esthetics.txt)

14. John Sculley, *Odyssey: Pepsi to Apple: The Journey of a Marketing Impresario* (New York: HarperCollins, 1987), p. 154.

15. John Sculley, personal interview, December 2007.

16. "The Guru: Steve Jobs," by Charles Arthur, *The Independent* (London, UK), Oct. 29, 2005.

17. "The Wired Interview: Steve Jobs: The Next Insanely Great Thing," by Gary Wolf, *Wired*, Issue 4.02, Feb. 1996.

18. "The Observer Profile: Father of Invention," by John Arlidge, *The Observer* (UK), Dec. 21, 2003.

19. Ibid.

20. Design Museum interview, March 29, 2007. (http://www .designmuseum.org/design/jonathan-ive)

21. Ibid.

22. "An Evening into Former Apple Industrial Designers," public lecture, June 4, 2007, Computer History Museum, Mountain View, California.

23. Ibid.

24. "Radical Craft: The Second Art Center Design Conference," by Janet Abrams, Core77 website, May 2007. (http://www.core77 .com/reactor/04.06__artcenter.asp)

25. "The Observer Profile."

26. "Radical Craft."

27. Jonathan Ive interview, by Marcus Fairs, iconeye, icon004, July/ Aug. 2003. (http://www.iconeye.com/articles/20070321__31)

28. "How Apple Does It," by Lev Grossman, *Time*, Oct. 16, 2005. (http://www.time.com/time/magazine/article/0,9171,1118384,00 .html)

29. Jonathan Ive interview, by Marcus Fairs.

30. "Radical Craft."

31. Jonathan Ive interview, by Marcus Fairs.

32. Ibid.

33. "Radical Craft."

34. Design Museum interview.

Chapter 4: Elitism: Hire Only *A* Players, Fire the Bozos

1. Smithsonian Institution Oral and Video Histories: "Steve Jobs."

2. Ibid.

3. "If He's So Smart … Steve Jobs, Apple, and the Limits of Innovation," by Carleen Hawn, *Fast Company*, Issue 78, Jan. 2004, p.68.

4. Brent Schlender, *Cases in Organizational Behavior* (Thousand Oaks, Calif.: Sage Publications, 2004), p. 206.

5. "How Pixar Adds a New School of Thought to Disney," by William C. Taylor and Polly LaBarre, *New York Times*, Jan. 29, 2006.

6. Ibid.

7. Smithsonian Institution Oral and Video Histories: "Steve Jobs."

8. "Joining the Mac Group," by Bruce Horn, Folklore.org. (http:/folklore.org/StoryView.py?project=Macintosh&story=Joining_the_Mac_Group.txt)

9. Essay by Steve Jobs in the premier issue of *Macworld* in 1984, p. 135. (http://www.macworld.com/2004/02/features/themacturns20jobs/)

10. *Rolling Stone*, April 4, 1996.

11. Smithsonian Institution Oral and Video Histories: "Steve Jobs."

12. Sculley, *Odyssey*, p. 87.

13. Geoffrey Moore, personal interview, October 2006.

14. "Dieter Rams," *Icon* Magazine, Feb. 2004.

15. Peter Hoddie, personal interview, September 2006.

16. "10 Years After '1984,'" by Bradley Johnson, *Advertising Age*, Jan. 10, 1994, pp. 1, 12–14.

17. "Apple Endorses Some Achievers Who 'Think Different,'" by Stuart Elliott, *New York Times*, Aug. 3, 1998.

18. "Here's to the Crazy Ones: The Crafting of 'Think Different,'" by Lee Clow and the Team at TBWA/Chiat/Day. (http://www.electric-escape.net/node/565)

19. Sculley, *Odyssey*, p. 108.

20. Ibid., p. 247.

21. Ibid., p. 191.

22. Ibid., p. 29.

23. Ibid.

24. "Apple Buffs Marketing Savvy to a High Shine," by Jefferson

Graham, *USA Today*, March 8, 2007. (http://www.usatoday
.com/tech/techinvestor/industry/2007-03-08-apple-marketing__
N.htm)

25. Warren Berger, personal interview, October 2006.
26. Seth Godin, personal interview, October 2006.
27. "I Hate Macs," by Charlie Booker, *The Guardian*, Feb. 5, 2007.
    (http://www.guardian.co.uk/commentisfree/story/0,,2006031,00
    .html)
28. "Monday Night at the Single's Club? Apple's Real People," by
    Andrew Orlowski, *The Register*, June 17, 2002. (http://www.the
    register.co.uk/2002/06/17/monday__night__at__the__singles/)
29. "Apple Endorses Some Achievers Who 'Think Different.' "
30. Ibid.

Chapter 5: Passion: Putting a Ding in the Universe

1. "Steve Jobs: The Rolling Stone Interview."
2. Edward Eigerman, personal interview, November 2007.
3. Sculley, *Odyssey*, p. 164.
4. Ibid., p. 165.
5. John Sculley, personal interview, December 2007.
6. "Triumph of the Nerds: How the Personal Computer Changed the
   World," PBS TV show, hosted by Robert Cringely, 1996. (http://
   www.pbs.org/nerds/part3.html)
7. Rama Dev Jager, *In the Company of Giants: Candid Conversations with
   the Visionaries of the Digital World* (Rafael Ortiz, 1997).
8. Upside.com, July 1998.
9. "The New, Improved Steve Jobs." Interview with Alan Deutschman,
   by Janelle Brown, Salon, Oct. 11, 2000. (http://dir.salon.com/
   story/tech/books/2000/10/11/deutschman/index1.html)
10. "Lessons Learned from Nearly Twenty Years at Apple," by David

Sobotta, Applepeels, Oct. 27, 2006. (http://viewfromthemountain
.typepad.com/applepeels/2006/10/lessons__learned.html)

Chapter 6: Inventive Spirit: Where Does the Innovation Come From?

1. "Apple Puts Power Mac G4 Cube on Ice." (http://www.apple.com/pr/library/2001/jul/03cube.html)
2. Andrew Orlowski in *The Register*, March 15, 2001. (http://www.theregister.co.uk/2001/03/15/apple__abandons__cube/)
3. "The Guts of a New Machine," by Rob Walker, *New York Times Magazine*, Nov. 30, 2003. (http://www.nytimes.com/2003/11/30/magazine/30IPOD.html)
4. Sculley, *Odyssey*, p. 285.
5. "The World's 50 Most Innovative Companies," *Business Week*. (http://bwnt.businessweek.com/interactive__reports/most__innovative/index.asp)
6. Jean Louis Gassée, *The Third Apple: Personal Computers and the Cultural Revolution* (Orlando, Fla.: Harcourt Brace Jovanovich, 1985), p. 115.
7. "Apple. Yes, Steve, You Fixed It. Congrats! Now What's Act Two?" by Peter Burrows with Jay Greene in Seattle, *Business Week*, July 31, 2000. (http://www.businessweek.com/2000/00__31/b3692001.htm)
8. AMR Research, "The 2007 Supply Chain Top 25," May 31, 2007. (http://www.amrresearch.com/content/view.asp?pmillid=20450)
9. "Steve Jobs: The Rolling Stone Interview."
10. "The Seed of Apple's Innovation," by Peter Burrows, *Business Week*, Oct. 12, 2004. (http://www.businessweek.com/bwdaily/dnflash/oct2004/nf20041012__4018__db083.htm)
11. Ibid.

12. Ibid.

13. "Global Innovation 1000," Booz Allen Hamilton, Oct. 17, 2007. (http://www.boozallen.com.au/media/image/Global__Innovation __1000__17Oct07.pdf)

14. "The Seed of Apple's Innovation."

15. "Steve Jobs: The Rolling Stone Interview."

16. "Steve Jobs at 44."

17. "Triumph of the Nerds."

18. Ibid.

19. "The Wired Interview: Steve Jobs."

20. Smithsonian Institution Oral and Video Histories: "Steve Jobs."

21. Sculley, *Odyssey*, p. 63.

22. John Sculley, personal interview, December 2007.

23. Sculley, *Odyssey*, p. 156.

24. "Steve Jobs at 44."

25. Jon Rubinstein, personal interview, October 2006.

26. Personal interview, October 2006

27. Jon Rubinstein, personal interview, October 2006.

28. Ibid.

29. Report of Ron Johnson's speech at the ThinkEquity Partners conference in San Francisco on Sept. 13, 2006, by Gary Allen. ifoAppleStore.com. (http://www.ifoapplestore.com/stores/ thinkequity__2006__rj.html)

30. Ibid.

31. "Commentary: Sorry, Steve: Here's Why Apple Stores Won't Work," by Cliff Edwards, *Business Week*, May 21, 2001.

32. "Apple: America's Best Retailer," by Jerry Useem, *Fortune*, March 8, 2007. (http://money.cnn.com/magazines/fortune/fortune__archive/ 2007/03/19/8402321/)

33. "The Stores," by Gary Allen, ifoAppleStore.com, Oct. 18, 2007. (http://www.ifoapplestore.com/the__stores.html)

34. Report of Ron Johnson's speech.

35. Ibid.
36. Ibid
37. "Apple Has a List of 100 Potential Store Sites," by Gary Allen, ifoAppleStore.com, April 27, 2004. (http://www.ifoapplestore.com/stores/risd__johnson.html)
38. "Apple: America's Best Retailer."
39. "Apple Has a List of 100 Potential Store Sites."
40. Report of Ron Johnson's speech.
41. "Apple Has a List of 100 Potential Store Sites."

Chapter 7: Case Study: How It All Came Together with the iPod

1. Personal interview, October 2006.
2. Macworld 2001 conference keynote.
3. "Detailed Analysis—Apple Warns: Inventories Still Growing, Lops 20% off 2001 Revenue Forecast," by Wes George, Dec. 6, 2000. (http://www.macobserver.com/article/2000/12/06.10.shtml)
4. Steven Levy, *The Perfect Thing: How the iPod Shuffles Commerce, Culture, and Coolness* (New York: Simon & Schuster, 2007), p. 29.
5. "iPod Nation," by Steven Levy, *Newsweek*, July 26, 2004. (http://www.newsweek.com/id/54529)
6. Jon Rubinstein, personal interview, September 2006.
7. "How Big Can Apple Get?"
8. "Apple's 21st-Century Walkman CEO Steve Jobs thinks he has something pretty nifty. And if he's right, he might even spook Sony and Matsushita," by Brent Schlender, *Fortune*, Nov. 12, 2001. (http://money.cnn.com/magazines/fortune/fortune__archive/2001/11/12/313342/index.htm)

Chapter 8: Total Control: The Whole Widget

1. "Steve Jobs, the iPhone and Open Platforms," by Dan Farber, ZDnet.com, Jan. 13, 2007.

2. "The Guts of a New Machine," by Rob Walker, *New York Times Magazine*, Nov. 30, 2003. (http:www.nytimes.com/2003/11/30/magazine/30IPOD.html)

3. "If He's So Smart ... Steve Jobs, Apple, and the Limits of Innovation," by Carleen Hawn, *Fast Company*, Issue 78, Jan. 2004, p. 68.

4. "Mea Culpa," by Andy Hertzfeld, Folklore.org. (http://www.folklore.org/StoryView.py?project=Macintosh&story=Mea__Culpa.txt)

5. "The Sansa-Rhapsody Connection," by James Kim, CNet Reviews, Oct. 5, 2006. (http://reviews.cnet.com/4520-6450__7-6648758-1.html)

6. "Apple Computer Is Dead; Long Live Apple," by Steven Levy, *Newsweek*, Jan. 10, 2007. (http://www.newsweek.com/id/52593)

7. "How Apple Does It."

8. "iPod Chief Not Excited About iTunes Phone," by Ed Oswald, *BetaNews*, Sept. 27, 2005 (http://www.betanews.com/article/iPod__Chief__Not__Excited__About__iTunes__Phone/1127851994?do=reply&reply__to=91676))

9. "Hardware and Software—The Lines Are Blurring," by Walt Mossberg, *All Things Digital*, April 30, 2007. (http://mossblog.allthingsd.com/20070430/hardware-software-success/)

10. "Getting in the game at Microsoft. Robbie Bach's job is to make software giant's entertainment division profitable," by Dan Fost and Ryan Kim, *San Francisco Chronicle*, May 28, 2007. (http://www.sfgate.com/cgi-bin/article.cgi?f=/c/a/2007/05/28/MICROSOFT.TMP)

11. "Sell digital experiences, not products. Solution boutiques will help consumers buy digital experiences," by Ted Schadler, Forrester

Research, Dec. 20, 2005. (http://www.forrester.com/Research/Document/Excerpt/0,7211,38277,00.html)

12. "Steve Jobs at 44."
13. "Hardware and Software."
14. "Steve Jobs at 44."
15. "How Big Can Apple Get?"

Index